CALIFORNIA HISTORY for Kids

Missions, Miners, and Moviemakers in the Golden State

Includes 21 Activities

KATY S. DUFFIELD

CHICAGO REVIEW PRESS

Library of Congress Cataloging-in-Publication Data

Duffield, Katy.
  California history for kids : missions, miners, and moviemakers in the Golden State ; 21 activities / Katy S. Duffield. — 1st ed.
    p. cm. — (For kids series)
  The earliest Californians — Shoebox archeological dig — Chumash rock painting — Miwok hoop and pole game — Early explorers and early settlers — Make an astrolabe — Sail a Spanish galleon — From Mexican California to an American beginning — Draw your own dise?o — Brand it! — Wave your flag — Gold! and statehood — Bake a hardtack snack — Create and send a letter sheet — Making connections — Whistle Morse code — Railroad cipher — Growing crops, growing cities — Grow a shasta daisy — Use-the-whole-orange muffins — Promote it! — A new century — Pack an earthquake preparedness kit — Become a backyard scientist — Produce your own movie — Hollywood handprints — Difficult times — Click! Create a photo essay — Moving forward — Make an air pollution logbook.
  ISBN 978-1-56976-532-6 (pbk.)
  1. California—History—Juvenile literature. 2. California—History—Study and teaching—Activity programs. I. Title.

F861.3.D84 2012
979.4—dc23

2011031471

Copyright © 2012 by Katy Duffield
All rights reserved
First edition
Published by Chicago Review Press, Incorporated
814 North Franklin Street
Chicago, Illinois 60610
ISBN 978-1-56976-532-6

Cover and interior design: Sarah Olson
Interior illustrations: Mark Baziuk
Cover photographs: Sequoias in Yosemite National Park, Galyna Andrushko/Shutterstock.com;
Golden Gate Bridge, Vacclav/Shutterstock.com; Grauman's Chinese Theater, Andy Z./Shutterstock.com;
Miner, Library of Congress LC-USZ62-13127; Mission San Luis Rey, Mariusz S. Jurgielewicz/Shutterstock.com.

Printed in the United States of America
10 9 8 7 6 5 4

Contents

Acknowledgments

I would like to offer my sincere thanks to the many people who have assisted me in this amazing journey. Throughout the project, Cindy Blobaum, Kerrie Hollihan, Katherine House, Pat McCarthy, Brandon Marie Miller, and many other NFforKids members offered advice and support. Shirley Anne Ramaley, Carla McClafferty, Nancy I. Sanders, and Leslie Duffield provided immeasurable help when it came to photos and permissions.

Additional thanks and hugs go to my incredible writer's group, the Ducks, who are *always* there with support and kind words: Shelly Becker, Kristy Dempsey, Alma Fullerton, Anne Marie Pace, Tanya Seale, and Cassandra Reigel Whetstone. Cassandra receives an extra-extra special thank-you for being my California connection and my critiquer extraordinaire!

I would also like to thank my editor, Jerome Pohlen, and all the great folks at Chicago Review Press, along with Mark Icanberry of LooLeDo.com. And last but not least, a big thanks to my family for always believing in me.

Time Line

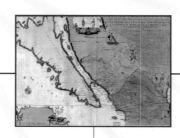

1.8 million–10,000 years ago	Pleistocene Epoch Ice Age begins
40,000–13,000 years ago	The first people cross over the Bering Land Bridge into North America
40,000–10,000 years ago	The last years of the Pleistocene Epoch; megafauna such as saber-toothed cats and mammoths roams California
15,000 years ago	Humans cross the Bering Land Bridge from Siberia to Alaska to become the "first Americans"
13,000–10,000 years ago	North American megafauna becomes extinct
Beginning 9,000 years ago	Native American population inhabits California
1535	Hernán Cortés sails to Baja (lower) California
1542	Juan Rodríguez Cabrillo becomes first European to enter San Diego Bay
1578	Sir Francis Drake claims California for England
1602	Sebastián Vizcaíno explores Monterey Bay, charts California coastline
1769	Father Serra establishes first mission at San Diego in Alta California
1776	Juan Bautista de Anza Party begins early California settlement

1821	Mexico achieves independence from Spain
1827	American trappers cross into California
1830s	Ranchos become established
1834	Secularization of missions begins
1841	Americans from the east begin arriving in California by wagon train
1841	William Wolfskill plants oranges in California
1846	United States declares war on Mexico
1848	US-Mexican War ends
1848	John Marshall discovers gold in Sierra foothills
1850	California becomes a state
1858	Overland Mail Company provides coast-to-coast mail delivery
1861	First cross-county telegraph message sent
1869	Transcontinental Railroad completed
1882	United States passes the Chinese Exclusion Act
1906	The San Francisco earthquake and fire

1910	First movie made in California
1913	Los Angeles Aqueduct completed
1920s	California Oil Boom
1929	Stock market crash begins Great Depression
1933	President Franklin D. Roosevelt introduces New Deal
1937	Golden Gate Bridge completed
1941	Japanese bomb Pearl Harbor
1942	Japanese Americans forced into internment camps
1955	Disneyland opens
1959	Los Angeles Dodgers are first California team to win the World Series
1964	SeaWorld opens
1965	César Chávez leads grape-picker strike
1971–72	Lakers win their first NBA World Championship Series since moving to L.A.
1977	Oakland Raiders become California's first Super Bowl winners

1984	Steve Jobs and Steve Wozniak introduce first Apple (Macintosh) computer
1989	Loma Prieta earthquake
1994	Northridge earthquake
2001	First statewide rolling blackouts
2001	Los Angeles Sparks bring home California's first WNBA championship
2002	Los Angeles Galaxy win their first MLS Cup
2002	Anaheim Angels win World Series
2003	Gray Davis recalled and Arnold Schwarzenegger elected governor
2003	Cedar wildfires devastate San Diego County
2006	Governor Schwarzenegger elected to a second term
2007	Witch wildfires inflame Santa Barbara County
2007	Anaheim Ducks win the Stanley Cup

Introduction

What's the first thing that comes to mind when you think about California? The glitz and glamour of Hollywood? Devastating earthquakes? Majestic redwoods? The technology of Silicon Valley? Mission bells? Beverly Hills? Disneyland? If you thought of any of these, you'd be right. Life in California is as rich and diverse as the people who have inhabited its land for centuries.

Even before the state of California existed as such, people the world over trekked to the area hoping for new opportunities and exciting discoveries. They looked at California as a place of richness and prosperity—a place where dreams could come true.

In the early 1500s, before the land now known as California was officially explored by Europeans, a Spanish author wrote of a mythical island located on the "right hand of the Indies" that overflowed with gold. According to the author, a beautiful queen named Calafia ruled a land inhabited only by black women. As European explorers made their way toward the region, this fabled land was no doubt in the back of their minds. Upon further investigation of the area, however, no land brimming with women was

(left) The bells at Mission San Juan Bautista as they looked in 1866. *Library of Congress, LC-USZ62-27578*

(right) Palm-lined street in Beverly Hills. *Library of Congress, LC-DIG-pplot-13725*

found, and explorers learned that California was not an island at all. Despite these facts, explorers still christened the land "California" as a tribute to Queen Calafia.

Throughout California's wide and varied history, people from all walks of life have visited or settled in the area for one reason or another. While the Spanish dreamed of riches and colonization, those from the eastern part of the United States saw California as a grand part of their nation. The first overland travelers, the gold rush forty-niners, and the Dust Bowl emigrants hoped California would provide better lives for them and their families. Later visitors longed for

the white-hot movie lights of Hollywood or the high-tech innovations of Silicon Valley. No matter what prompted people to travel to and settle in California, it's safe to assume that each came looking for golden opportunities.

Today, around 37 million people call California home—a greater population than any other US state. Strong and resilient residents from all backgrounds who have called California home for hundreds of years, along with those arriving in the Golden State for the very first time, remain determined to chase the dreams that brought them there.

CALIFORNIA FAST FACTS

Capital	Sacramento
State Nickname	The Golden State
State Motto	Eureka!
Entered Union	September 9, 1850
Population (2010)	37,253,956
Percentage of population under 18 years old	25.5%
Total Land Area	163,695.5 square miles *(Third largest in the United States)*
Length of Coastline	1,264 miles
Highest Point	Mount Whitney *14,495 feet (Highest point in contiguous United States)*
Lowest Point	Badwater, in Death Valley *282 feet below sea level (Lowest elevation point in the United States)*
Largest City	Los Angeles *(Second largest city in the United States)*
Second Largest City	San Diego
National Park Acreage	4.1 million acres
Miles of Public Roads	169,905.53 miles
Number of Dentist Offices (2008)	20,156
Number of Fast-Food Restaurants (2008)	35,309
Number of Amusement Parks (2008)	49
Number of Active Volcanoes	3
Average Number of Earthquakes a Year Strong Enough to Be Felt	100–150

State Seal of California. *National Oceanic and Atmospheric Administration/ Department of Commerce*

A California redwood; note the man standing at its base. *Library of Congress LC-USZ62-132177*

1

The Earliest Californians

In order to appreciate California's rich history, it's important to start at the beginning. Go back, way back, to the Ice Age at the end of the Pleistocene epoch (PLYS-tuh-seen EH-puck), 40,000 to 10,000 years ago. Humans have yet to set foot in the area.

At first glance, the land might have appeared totally desolate, but a wide variety of interesting creatures did in fact exist among the sage scrub, pine, and cypress.

A Sticky Situation

An extraordinary spot in Southern California boasts of one of the most plentiful deposits of Ice Age fossils in the world. Rancho La Brea (ran-CHO lah BRAY-uh), often referred to as the "tar pits," is found within Hancock Park near the heart of Los Angeles. A single glance tells visitors they are looking at something quite unusual. Softball-sized globs bubble to the top of a pool of gooey, dark gunk.

Even though it's often called "tar," the gunk in the La Brea Pits is actually asphalt. The pits form when crude oil creeps to the earth's surface through cracks called fissures. After the lighter portions of the oil evaporate, only the heavier oil, or asphalt, remains, creating the sticky pools. Each day, about 8 to 12 gallons (32 to 48 liters) of oil ooze to the surface.

Yurock man in a canoe on the Trinity River.
Library of Congress, LC-USZ62-118588

These pits may be interesting, but what do they have to do with California *history*? Plenty. Bones found in these gummy pits have provided vital clues to California's very first inhabitants.

When people first began finding bones in the asphalt pools, they didn't think the remains were anything unusual—they simply thought the bones came from cattle that had wandered into the pits and become stuck. In 1901, however, scientists began excavating the site, performing tests, and reconstructing skeletons of the retrieved bones. At that point they learned the remains came from animals that made up a part of California's ancient past.

From early excavation to the present day, scientists have recovered the remains of 231 different species of vertebrates, 234 types of invertebrates, and more than 150 types of plants. And these aren't simply animals we recognize today; the remains include bones from extinct creatures such as dire wolves, saber-toothed cats, ground sloths, Columbian mammoths, American mastodons, and many more.

If you've ever stepped into a mud hole so deep and sticky that you've almost lost your shoe trying to get your foot out, you have a sense of what birds, coyotes, American lions, frogs, turtles, ancient bison, short-faced bears, and others went through when they stepped on or were chased into one of the asphalt pits. In warm temperatures, the asphalt pools became extremely sticky. Sometimes leaves, dust, and water covered the pits, camouflaging the danger that lurked below. Insects, birds, and small mammals might have become immediately trapped on contact with the asphalt. Larger animals might have sunk only a few inches into the asphalt's stickiness but fought back hard enough to escape. Still others struggled until exhaustion forced them to surrender to the gooey mass. And in some cases, predators attacked prey that were already trapped—only to become entrapped themselves.

Dire wolves, mammals similar to modern timber wolves, are the most commonly discovered large mammal fossils in the pits. More than 3,000 have been found in the La Brea Pits. The saber-toothed cat, the official state fossil of California, is the second most commonly discovered fossil. In total, more than one million bones have been recovered from the pits. These discoveries have provided vital information about the types of creatures that once roamed California.

These creatures were the first to tromp across ancient California, but where did California's first humans come from?

WHAT'S IN A NAME?

The word *brea* means "tar" in Spanish, so when someone says "La Brea Tar Pits," what they're actually saying is "the tar tar pits." The pits' name probably made little difference to the only human whose remains were found in the asphalt pools. Excavators discovered the skull, jawbone, and left thighbone of the La Brea Woman in 1914. Scientists used special testing methods called radiocarbon dating to determine that the remains were 9,000 years old.

SHOEBOX ARCHAEOLOGICAL DIG

Teams at the La Brea Pits continue to search for clues to life of long ago. Paleontologists at La Brea and scientists in other areas of California carefully excavate specific areas in search of fossils. This activity will give you an idea about the work they do.

Materials

Shoebox, or other box, about 4 inches deep
Marker
Helper
Ruler
Sand
A variety of small items such as coins, buttons, sunflower seeds, dried beans, dry pasta, beads, etc.
Store-bought potting soil
Soil dug from outside
Scissors
String
Plastic spoon
Small paintbrush
Paper
Pencil
Blank, self-stick labels
Snack-sized plastic bags

☛ Cover your workspace with a newspaper. On the short end of a shoebox, write an N for North and on the opposite end write S for South. With the S facing toward you, write E for East on the right side and W for West on the left side.

While you're not watching, ask a helper to fill the shoebox in the following manner: Add about half an inch of sand to the bottom of the box. Place four or five objects in various areas of the sand layer, then add half an inch of the potting soil on top of the objects and sand. Next, place four or five objects in the potting soil layer, then add about half an inch of soil dug from the ground outside on top of the potting soil layer. Finally, put four or five objects in this top layer and cover them with more outside soil.

Use scissors to cut a small slit into the center of each short end of the shoebox. Cut a length of string about six inches longer than the length of the box. Place one end of the string into each slit, leaving a "tail" of string on each end. Tie a knot in each end of the string

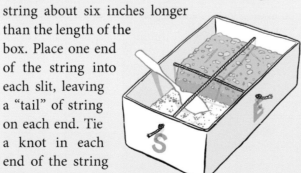

close to the box to prevent the string from slipping. Repeat these steps on the long sides of the box. These strings create your quadrant grid.

Begin your excavation in one particular quadrant (northeast, northwest, southeast, or southwest) set out by your string lines. On a sheet of paper, record which quadrant you'll excavate first. Using a plastic spoon, carefully dig through *only* the top layer of material.

If you find an item, clean it off carefully with a paintbrush. Place the item in a baggie and label the baggie with the date and time the object was discovered, along with the quadrant and layer details of where the item was found. Continue excavating in all four quadrants until you have cleared off the top layer.

RECORD SHEET				
Date	Time	Quadrant	Layer	Item
5-3-11	4:25 PM	Southwest	Top	Coin

Next, work through the middle layer and finally the bottom layer. Record everything you've uncovered.

California's First Human Inhabitants

A debate rages over the identities of the first people to set foot in the Americas and how they arrived there. Some archaeologists believe the first Americans came from northeast Asia, while others believe the first inhabitants arrived from Australia, Southeast Asia, or South America. As to how these first Americans arrived, some researchers say by foot; others say it was by boat. Archaeologists continue to study evidence both old and new in order to learn as much as possible about the identity of the "first Americans."

TIGER OR CAT?

Some people mistakenly call the saber-toothed cat a saber-toothed "tiger." Due to its bobbed tail, shorter body length, and heavier body weight, scientists do not consider this ancient animal to be closely related to the tiger. Instead, they regard it as a saber-toothed "cat" instead.

Evidence suggests that rather than chasing its prey like a tiger might, a saber-toothed cat hid, and then ambushed its victims. It used its substantial body weight to hold down its prey, then sunk its eight-inch-long teeth into the prey's throat or belly area. Researchers believe saber-tooths didn't use their long teeth to rip or tear a prey animal's body because this method could easily break a cat's teeth or even its skull!

Saber-toothed cat skull.
iStockphoto.com/David Rose

The traditional theory behind the coming of the first Americans revolves around a land called Beringia. During the late Pleistocene Ice Age a huge amount of ocean water became frozen into huge, flowing ice sheets called glaciers, which caused sea levels to drop. This drop exposed land that had been previously covered by water. One such land area, called Beringia, emerged from the Bering Strait, a channel of water located between Siberia and present-day Alaska. Some archaeologists believe that people migrated to North America between 40,000 and 13,000 years ago by walking from Siberia to Alaska across what is known as the Bering Land Bridge.

When picturing a "land bridge," it's easy to imagine a narrow strip of land, but scientists don't believe that is accurate when it comes to the Bering Land Bridge. They estimate that the grassy, treeless plain ranged up to 1,000 miles wide. But no matter what it's called, many archaeologists

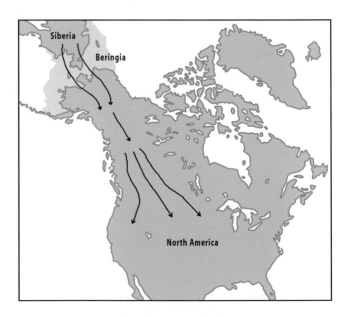

now agree that the first Americans crossed this land area from Asia to populate the Americas.

These first human inhabitants of North America, thought to be hunter-gatherers, may have followed mammoth, mastodon, and other large-bodied animals called megafauna across the land bridge from Siberia to North America. Eventually these first inhabitants made their way to other areas. Experts aren't sure of the exact routes taken during the migration. Some believe early inhabitants moved southward and settled in present-day California, while others believe they first migrated east toward the plains and later drifted back into California. Still others believe that coastal migration (arrival by water routes) took place. Theories of people arriving by boat are still being studied. Unfortunately, the rise in sea levels that occurred since the last Ice Age flooded much of California's coastline, taking with it important archaeological evidence.

The Arlington Springs Woman's age (see sidebar) adds another piece to the "how and when" puzzle of the arrival of the first Americans. Traditional Bering Land Bridge theories established that the first settlers had possibly arrived in North America about 11,500 years ago. The dating of the remains of the Arlington Springs Woman, along with the fact that her bones were found on an island, support conflicting theories. Maybe early inhabitants *did* arrive by boat, and perhaps they arrived much earlier than first believed.

No matter how they arrived, the first people of the Americas—called Paleo-Indians, which means "old Indians"—did, in fact, reach California as early as 20,000 years ago. Over time,

THE ARLINGTON SPRINGS WOMAN

Some of the oldest human remains ever found in North America were discovered on California's Channel Islands. Two thigh bones of the Arlington Springs Woman, as she became known, were found in 1959 at a site called Arlington Springs on California's Santa Rosa Island. At that time, sufficient technologies weren't available to accurately date the remains so scientists had to wait more than 30 years to find out the approximate age of the Arlington Springs bones. In the late 1990s experts used DNA and a method called radiocarbon dating to estimate the skeletal remains' age to be 13,000 years old.

the cultures of these earliest people continued to evolve, and they began to leave evidence of their lives behind for archaeologists to discover. Items such as spear points, baskets, stone bowls, and beads have been excavated from California sites. Archaeologists study these items to determine how they might have been used. They also study the various villages in which these early Californians lived. These studies allow researchers to better understand the lives of the earliest people, the Paleo-Indians, and their descendants, the early Native Americans.

Village Life

Many of the first California Native Americans lived in small village groups of about 100 to 500 people. Sometimes, several smaller communities combined made up larger villages. These villages often surrounded a large building called a roundhouse that sat in the center of a main village.

Whenever the native peoples needed to discuss problems they met at the roundhouse. They also held celebrations in the building.

One interesting use of the roundhouse by the Maidu (MAY-doo) tribe of central California was the grizzly bear dance. The Maidu people believed if they honored grizzlies with a dance and feast, the animals wouldn't attack their people. Even today, the Maidu people continue to perform different types of cultural dances.

Many Native American villages also had a building called a sweat lodge The sweat lodge was made by building a wooden structure above a large hole in the ground. To enter, native men (women were not usually allowed in) climbed down a ladder into the earthen hole. Once inside, they built a fire so that the room would become very warm. As you might guess by its name, the sweathouse was a place the men went to sweat.

Men of the Miwok (MEE-wuk) and other tribes used the sweat lodge before hunting or important ceremonies (and some still do). Miwok men sat in the scorching house, sweat dripping. After as much as three hours inside, the men quickly climbed the ladder and raced outside to jump into a pool of cool water. After that, they sometimes went back in and did it all over again. The men believed this ritual was good for cleanliness and health, and that it purified them and helped them become better hunters.

Outside of the main villages, California's early Native Americans built their own individual houses. As in other parts of their lives, the natives considered the climate and resources that surrounded them before building their homes.

The Yurok tribe of the northwest Pacific coast had just what they needed to build their homes. Huge redwood trees located near their villages made the perfect building material for constructing their split-plank homes.

The Mountain Maidu had to think about the snow and freezing temperatures in their areas when building their homes. The Mountain Maidu dug two- to three-foot-deep holes and then built

CHUMASH ROCK PAINTING

A stunning look back at early Native American history exists in the hills above present-day Santa Barbara. Hundreds of years ago the Chumash created colorful, imaginative cave rock art. The Chumash painted designs on the rock using pigments from nearby minerals like hematite (red), charcoal (black), and gypsum (white) mixed with water, plant juices, or animal fat.

No one knows exactly how to decipher the symbols, but many believe the human and animal images, circles, squiggles, and lines may have been painted by shamans to honor the spiritual world. Today, visitors can view some of the rock art by visiting the Chumash Painted Cave State Historic Park north of Santa Barbara (www.parks.ca.gov/?page_id=602).

CHUMASH ROCK PAINTING

Try your hand at making a rock painting.

Materials

Long, flat rock, about 3 inches
    by 6 inches
Acrylic paints: red, white,
    and/or black
Paintbrushes
Small, straight twig
Safety goggles

☞ Find a rock about the size of your fist. Wash it thoroughly so that the paint will stick to it.

When the rock is fully dry, choose a Chumash design or two and decide how you want it to appear on your rock. You may want to lightly sketch the design on the rock before painting. Use the traditional red, white, or black Chumash colors to paint your design.

You can paint using a regular paintbrush or try something a little more authentic. The Chumash did not have paintbrushes like we use today. Some researchers believe the Chumash may have used twigs to paint their designs. If you want to give this a try, find a straight twig, about the length of a regular paintbrush. Put on your safety goggles and then place the twig on a hard outside surface such as a concrete driveway. Using the fist-sized rock as a hammer, tap the end of the twig until it fans out into a brush-like formation. Try your hand at using this "brush" to paint your design. Think of how long it must have taken to paint the murals on the walls of the caves!

Tule shelter on Lake Pomo.
Library of Congress,
LC-USZ62-98673

Food

Most California Native Americans that lived during this time were hunter-gatherers. They scoured woodlands for berries, grasses, nuts, and acorns; hunted for game such as deer, elk, and rabbits; and fished the waterways for salmon, crab, and clams. A few groups grew crops, and some even nibbled on grasshoppers, caterpillars, and seaweed.

Since some of the Chumash tribes lived on islands or in coastal areas, they not only hunted inland game, such as squirrel and geese, but also ocean game. Chumash hunters rowed out in canoes called *tomols* (TOH-mohlz) to harpoon seals, sea otters, and even porpoises.

The Karok, whose name means "upriver people," feasted on the salmon and steelhead they caught from the Klamath River. The Karok had an interesting way of catching fish: they hung nets from platforms built over the river, and as the salmon leaped from the water when traveling upstream, they jumped right into the nets. This method was so effective that several days of fishing often provided enough food for the tribe for the entire winter. It only had to be cured by drying or smoking first.

Like other tribes, the Cahuilla hunted game and gathered other edible materials, but they also planted their own food for harvest. The Cahuilla tended to plants that already grew in the area, such as cactus (which they boiled and ate) and mesquite beans (that they pounded into meal), but they also grew crops. Squash, corn, melons, and beans could all be found growing near Cahuilla villages.

their homes over and around each hole. The ground helped to insulate their houses from the cold. They also built steeply slanted rooftops so that heavy snowfalls would slide off more easily.

Other tribes, such as the Chumash, built dome-shaped houses roofed with grass mats, while some Cahuilla (ka-WEE-ya) families made their homes by simply sheltering the front of a cave with a tangle of brush.

Fish, plants, and wildlife were important foods in the lives of the early native people, but out of everything they ate, one thing stands out as a primary food source: the acorn. Abundant oak trees such as the blue oak, black oak, valley oak, and tanbark oak provided the natives with huge amounts of acorns, which are rich in fat and energy-providing carbohydrates. Most tribes ate acorn meal daily in the form of mush, soup, or bread. One source notes that in some Maidu cultures, an adult could eat up to a ton of acorns each year—that's 2,000 pounds of acorns!

In autumn, acorn harvesting time, young men and boys climbed high into the oak trees. Some of them shook the trees' limbs to make the acorns fall. Others knocked the acorns to the ground by hitting the trees' branches with poles. Women, children, and the elderly scurried on the ground below, gathering the fallen acorns and placing them in baskets. The acorns were dried in the sun and then stored in granaries, large shelters made from woven grasses, twigs, and vines. Granaries, built on stilts so that the acorns would be stored above the ground to keep animals and other pests from destroying or gobbling up crop, could each hold between 100 to 1,000 pounds of acorns.

Trade

Traders from one tribe might visit another to swap some of their own plentiful resources for items their region lacked. Salt, fish, acorns, tools, and skins were all traded between groups.

In some northern Miwok villages a volcanic glass called obsidian could be found. The Miwok

CHEMUCK CHOW DOWN

Preparing acorns for eating was a long, drawn-out process. First, the women of the tribe removed the acorns from their shells. Then they pounded them with heavy stones to make a ground-up substance called meal. Next, the meal had to be soaked to remove the tannin, an ingredient that makes acorns bitter. To remove the tannin, the women used special containers called leaching baskets. Women placed leaves in the bottom of the loosely woven baskets, added the meal, and repeatedly poured water over it. This allowed the water to run through, but kept the meal safely inside. When the meal turned white the tannin was removed, and the meal was ready to be cooked into soup, bread, or a mush called *chemuck*.

To cook *chemuck*, women placed a mixture of meal and water into special baskets made for cooking. The cook then carefully slid heated rocks into the mixture and began stirring. She stirred and stirred until the heat from the rocks cooked the mush. To spice up the finished product, some tribes added berries, herbs, dried fish, or even cedar bark to the nutty-flavored *chemuck*.

Acorn storage granaries in Yosemite Valley.
Library of Congress, LC-USZ62-86249

chipped the shiny black stones into strong, efficient arrow points. Since obsidian wasn't available in all areas, it was a valuable item that could be traded to other groups for various goods.

Instead of trading goods, some tribes used shells as money. The Pomo exchanged clamshells or clamshell beads with other groups for fish. The Yurock and Hupa prized a different type of shell called dentalium. Yurocks strung the long, thin shells on lengths of string and used them for currency. A small boat might be purchased for a 13-bead string, while a house could cost 2 strings; obsidian blades ranged from 2 to 10 strings. Ceremony dancers or important people in the community might wear the shell beads on elaborate necklaces or to decorate their clothing—the amount of dentalium worn often signified how wealthy, famous, or important a person was.

(right) Northwestern California Hupa woman wearing dentalium beads. *Library of Congress, LC-USZ62-101261*

(below) California Native American basketry. *Library of Congress, LC-USZ62-98667*

Basketry

Baskets played another important part of daily village life. Native American women created baskets from willow twigs, grasses, roots, and other materials. They also used tule, a plant similar to the cattail. Baskets woven in sizes ranging from the tiniest cups, to bowls, to larger storage containers were designed to fit different uses. And the baskets weren't just useful; many were beautiful as well. The Pomo often made coiled baskets in which grass or twig bundles were stitched together, while other groups such as the Maidu primarily made twined baskets.

Native people used burden baskets to collect acorns or other foods. Other baskets, used for cooking such foods as acorn mush, had to be waterproof. Skilled basket weavers could weave baskets tightly enough that no water would leak through. The Maidu sometimes used pine tar or asphaltum, such as that found in the La Brea Pits, to waterproof their baskets. Food was also stored in baskets. Some baskets weren't used for food at all; some were used as small packages for gifts or to hold valuables, and others were worn as hats to protect the wearers' heads from the sun.

California Native Americans wisely utilized the resources that California's varied geography offered them. They had a great respect for the natural world and worked to give back the resources they used. They wanted to make sure these resources would be available to their children and to their children's children. What the Native Americans may not have known is that they would soon share their world with those from outside their tribes.

ACTIVITY ▶ MIWOK HOOP-AND-POLE GAME

The Miwok played many different games. One popular pastime was the hoop-and-pole game. This version will use beanbags instead of poles.

Materials

2 players
Hula hoop
Beanbags

☞ Since you will be rolling the hoop on its side, you'll need to find a large, level playing area, either indoors or outdoors.

Players should stand about three to five feet apart. Player 1, the "roller," holds the hoop at one end of the playing area. Player 2, the "thrower," stands to the roller's side, facing in the same direction. The roller then rolls the hoop forward on its end, while the thrower tries to toss a bean bag through the moving hoop.

If the thrower is successful, the thrower scores one point. Then, players switch places to allow the other person to throw. The first player to score 10 points wins.

To make the game more difficult, the thrower can move a farther distance from the roller.

2

Early Explorers and Early Settlers

For thousands of years, Paleo-Indians and Native Americans were the only people living in California. By the late 1400s and early 1500s, however, changes began to take place. People from other countries began to take interest in the West. Two of those countries were England and Spain. Adventurers wished to explore and conquer new areas and claim them for their own countries. Spanish conquistadors and English explorers hoped to find new sea routes that could make their voyages to Asia shorter. They also hoped to find lands of plentiful resources and maybe even riches and fame.

Hernán Cortés

Spanish conquistador Hernán Cortés (kor-TEZ) is most well known as the conqueror of the Aztec empire of Mexico for Spain, a colony that was part of the territory known as New Spain. But Cortés had California connections as well. From 1527 to 1539 Cortés led or sponsored several voyages to explore parts of the Pacific Ocean. Cortés hoped to find additional lands to conquer for Spain. He also hoped to discover a fabled waterway that connected the Atlantic and Pacific Oceans that the Spanish called the Strait of Anián (ah-nee-AHN).

Cortés and others believed this waterway existed in northern North America. If Cortés could find the strait, also known as the Northwest Passage, he and his ships could save an enormous amount of time when sailing from Europe to Asia. Cortés had also heard stories of a rich and marvelous land located to the northwest. He dreamed of further fame and riches to be found if he could locate the rumored cities that were said to be full of gold, silver, rubies, and pearls.

In the mid-1530s Cortés led an expedition northward from Acapulco. In 1535 he landed on the shores of La Paz, situated on the eastern shore of the present-day Gulf of California. Cortés had discovered the peninsula of Baja (BAH-hah), or "lower," California. At La Paz he established a base from which land exploration could be conducted.

Cortés spent two hopeful years in the hot, dry area, but the only riches he found were pearls from the oysters in the waters off the coast. The outpost at La Paz was soon abandoned, but Cortés and other Spanish explorers did not completely lose hope of finding wealth in the new land.

Juan Rodríguez Cabrillo

Seven years after Cortés landed at Baja, Portuguese explorer Juan Rodríguez Cabrillo (cah-BREE-yoh) set out on his journey to the Pacific. In June 1542 Cabrillo departed from the port of Navidad, near modern-day Manzanillo, Mexico. His mission was to search for the mythical Strait of Anián that Cortés had also sought. Along the way, Cabrillo and his men would also explore the northwest coast of the continent.

Cabrillo's flagship, the *San Salvador*, and a small secondary ship, the *Victoria*, carried crews of sailors, slaves, a priest, livestock, and enough

(left) Portrait of Hernán Cortés (1485–1547). *Library of Congress, LC-USZ62-33515*

(right) View of Baja. *Library of Congress, LC-DIG-pga-01397*

supplies to last two years. Some sources note that Cabrillo's ships were relatively small, poorly built, and severely lacking the supplies needed to carry out such a journey. But this did not stop Cabrillo, who was considered a brave and experienced navigator.

On September 28, 1542, Cabrillo discovered "a closed and very good harbor" and became the first European to enter what became known as San Diego Bay. He was the first European to set foot in modern-day California.

As Cabrillo and his men continued northward, they may have been the first Europeans to encounter California's Native Americans. At one area close to the Santa Barbara Channel, Cabrillo noted a village, possibly Chumash, situated on the coast. Since such a large number of *tomols,* or canoes, dotted the village area, Cabrillo and his men named the spot *Pueblo de las Canoas*, or the Town of the Canoes.

For the most part, the Native Americans that he and his crew met were friendly. At one stopover, native people pointed the crew to a watering hole so the sailors could replenish their water supplies. In another location, the natives supplied the travelers with sardines.

On Christmas Eve 1542, Cabrillo was injured. Sources do not agree, but Cabrillo broke either his arm or leg in either a fall or in a skirmish with Native Americans. Cabrillo's injury did not stop the expedition, however. The explorers continued northward and made their way as far as Point Reyes, just beyond San Francisco. Strong northwest winds and rough seas forced the expedition to turn back southward.

MAJOR MAP MISTAKE

Before anyone they knew had undertaken an in-depth exploration of the California coastlines, many mapmakers, called cartographers, believed that the present-day Gulf of California was not a gulf at all. They thought California was completely surrounded by water: they thought it was an island.

It wasn't until 1700, when Jesuit missionary and cartographer Eusebio Kino explored the Gulf of California, that the California island myth began to crumble. But for another 40 years people continued to insist that California was completely separated by water from the mainland. It took a royal decree from Spain's King Ferdinand VII in 1747 to settle the issue once and for all. The king declared, "California is not an island."

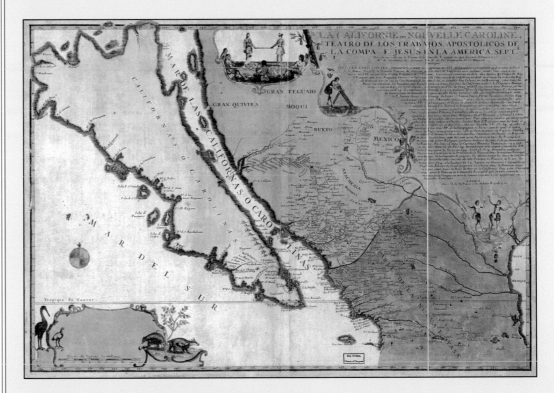

Map of California when it was still believed to be an island.
Library of Congress, G4410 1720 .F42 TIL Vault

Along this journey, Cabrillo's wound worsened. He suffered from gangrene, an infection that would cause his death on January 3, 1543. Before he died, Cabrillo made his chief pilot promise to continue northward. Cabrillo's crew followed his wishes, and the expedition made its way to the present-day California-Oregon border before heading home to Navidad in April 1543. Though no one knows the exact location, Cabrillo is believed to have been buried on one the islands off California, possibly San Miguel or Santa Rosa.

Portrait of Sir Francis Drake (1540–96). *Library of Congress, LC-USZ62-38479*

Francis Drake

For many years after Cabrillo's voyage, the Spanish lost interest in California. Cabrillo's expedition had brought back no promising news that would warrant additional voyages at that time. In the late 1500s, however, another country took interest in and visited California's coast. England's Queen Elizabeth I sent sea captain Francis Drake on a round-the-world voyage in late 1577.

Relations between England and Spain during this time were poor, to say the least. As he made his way around the world, Drake acted as a pirate. He seized Spanish ships and robbed them of their silver and other treasure. When he reached the Pacific Ocean almost a year and a half later, Drake's ship, the *Golden Hinde*, was in bad shape. Weighted down with about 30 tons of stolen Spanish treasure, the ship was literally splitting at its hull's seams. On June 17, 1579, Drake navigated the ailing ship into a bay on the Point Reyes peninsula, known today as Drake's Bay. The vessel remained anchored for five weeks while repairs were made.

Before setting off again, Drake claimed California for England and christened it *Nova Albion*, or New England. At Point Reyes, he left behind a brass plate attached to a wooden post to observe the achievement. A silver sixpence adorned with Queen Elizabeth's image was set into a small hole carved into the plate. Unfortunately, the monument no longer exists, but even so, England had made its first mark upon California.

Upon Drake's return to England in September 1580, about three years after his departure,

MAKE AN ASTROLABE

Spanish explorers of the early 16th century, such as Hernán Cortés and Juan Cabrillo, may have used an astrolabe to help guide them on their journeys. The instrument measures the altitude of the sun or stars to help determine latitude, a measurement of a location's distance from the equator.

Materials

Drinking straw
Scissors
Large plastic protractor
Tape
String, about 12 inches long
A metal washer (a bolt or an
    old key with a hole in the
    top works too)
Pencil
Paper
1 sheet of black
    construction paper
1 helper
3–5 sunny days

☛ Cut a drinking straw so it is the same length as the flat portion of your protractor. Tape the straw at each end of the flat side so that the straw rests on the thin edge of the protractor.

Tie a string around the center of the flat side of the protractor. (Some protractors have a small hole in the center of the flat side. If so, you can tie your string there.) Make sure that the string hangs down the very center of the numbered side of the protractor. Tie your washer to the other end of the string.

You can use your astrolabe to measure the altitude (the location) of the sun. *Remember: never look directly at the sun, as it can damage your eyes.* In this activity, you will not be looking at the sun.

First, record the date and time of your observation on paper. Now, with the curved part of the protractor facing downward, point one end of the straw toward the sun. Ask your helper to hold the construction paper under the astrolabe so that you can see its shadow. Move the

astrolabe around until you can see a small circle of light coming through the straw onto the construction paper. When this occurs, you will know that the protractor is pointed directly at the sun. This step can be a little tricky, but by watching the shadow of the straw on the paper you should be able to line it up.

Once the sunlight passes through the straw, either ask your helper to read the number on the protractor where the string rests, or slide your finger down the string and hold it in place while you read the measurement. Record your measurement.

Obtain measurements at the same time of day for three to five days, or even a week. Record them. What did you discover? Did your measurements change? Did they increase or decrease? The change in the sun's altitude is caused by the tilt of the earth's axis. In the springtime, your readings should increase as the days go by. In autumn, they will decrease.

Queen Elizabeth knighted him Sir Francis Drake for his efforts in support of England.

Sebastián Vizcaíno

Sir Francis Drake's voyage to California renewed Spain's interest in the area. The Spanish realized that it was important for them to establish ports and settlements in the region before another country beat them to it. It was also important for Spanish ships traveling from Manila to Acapulco to have a sheltered port where they could obtain fresh supplies before continuing on their journeys.

The viceroy of New Spain, the man appointed to rule Spain's colony, chose Sebastián Vizcaíno, a merchant-adventurer, to lead an expedition to California. The Spanish government wanted Vizcaíno to locate a port for settlement and to accurately map the California coastline. Vizcaíno also had orders that he was not to change the names of previously identified landmarks, an order he later ignored.

On May 5, 1602, Vizcaíno and his men set sail from Acapulco with three small ships including his flagship, the *San Diego*. Six months later, on November 10, Vizcaíno arrived at the area Cabrillo had named San Miguel. Vizcaíno immediately renamed the bay San Diego.

Why would he have changed the name after being ordered not to? Some historians believe Vizcaíno simply ignored the viceroy's orders. Others, however, think the maps from earlier expeditions Vizcaíno used were so poorly drawn that it was impossible for Vizcaíno to follow

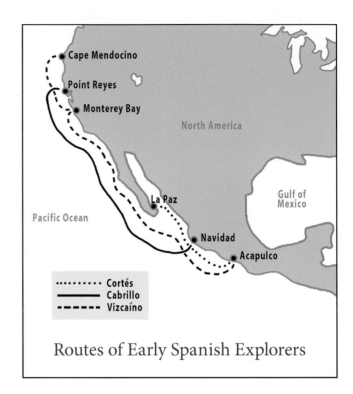

Routes of Early Spanish Explorers

them—he simply had no way of knowing if he was visiting the same areas as those who came before him or someplace completely new.

From San Diego, Vizcaíno continued northward up the coast until he came to a bay he named to honor the Spanish viceroy, the Conde de Monterey, or Count of Monterey. Vizcaíno wrote glowingly about Monterey Bay, which he described as "the best port that one could hope for" in that it was "sheltered from all winds." Vizcaíno also raved about the fertile soil, abundance of trees with which ships could be built or repaired, and the great quantity of wildlife that existed there.

Some later questioned Vizcaíno's assessment of Monterey Bay. Many who came after him saw the bay as a poorly sheltered harbor. But if this were true, why would Vizcaíno mislead the viceroy? Perhaps Vizcaíno believed if he did not return with a favorable report, he would not receive the rewards the viceroy had promised him for a successful journey.

First European Settlers

After Vizcaíno's voyage, no further Spanish expeditions explored the California coast for more than 160 years. Why did they wait so long to return? The Spanish simply did not have the money or the manpower to undertake an extensive settlement. The Spanish view changed, however, after Russia entered the picture.

In the late 18th century, Russian traders began making their way southward along the coast from Alaska. Russian fur traders hunting sea otters and seals for pelts became a threat to the Spanish—what if they settled in California first and claimed the land for Russia? Even though both Spain and England had laid claim to the land in the 1500s, neither country had built colonies, so they both felt California was still open for the taking. Leaders of these countries and others did not stop to consider whether the native people already living in California had any claim on the land.

Russia's threat set Spain in motion. In order to protect their interests in the area, the leaders of Spain decided to use the Pious Fund—donations made by individuals and religious groups—to finance a settlement expedition. In 1769 a Spanish inspector general, a priest, and a soldier set out on a mission to settle Alta California.

SCURVY

Voyagers during Vizcaíno's time had plenty to worry about—pirates, foul weather, hostile natives, strong ocean currents, and illness. One particularly dangerous illness was scurvy. Scurvy is caused by a lack of vitamin C. On the lengthy voyages sailors often traveled in the 15th and 16th centuries, fruits and vegetables were rarely stocked. Since there was no way of keeping produce from spoiling on these months- or year-long journeys, sailors often did not eat enough foods that contained vitamin C to keep them healthy. Scurvy sufferers experienced such dreadful symptoms as swollen and bleeding gums, lost teeth, weakness, diarrhea, muscle and joint pain, and bruising. If left untreated, the illness could also cause death.

During their 1602 voyage, as many as 40 of Vizcaíno's men may have died from scurvy. At one point on the trip home, Vizcaíno hoped to stop at Monterey but was afraid that, if they dropped anchor, his sickened crew would not be strong enough to pull it up again. Fortunately, sailors later discovered that drinking lemon or lime juice could keep them from getting the illness.

SAIL A SPANISH GALLEON

Many of the Spanish explorers traveled in ships called galleons. Try your hand at making a galleon model.

Adult supervision required

Materials

½-gallon square paper milk carton (not plastic)
Ruler
Pen
Knife
Scissors
Masking tape
Newspaper
Drinking straws
Hole punch
White plastic shopping bag
String
Colored markers, if desired

☞ Rest the milk carton on its side. Measure about 1½ inches from each corner and mark with a pen. Ask an adult to begin cutting at each mark and cut at an angle as shown. Repeat on other side until the center piece comes out. Even out the cut lines with scissors.

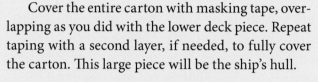

Trim any rough edges from the piece you just removed from the carton. This will be the ship's lower deck. Use masking tape to cover the lower deck. Overlapping the masking tape strips will give the deck a "boarded" look. With a knife or the end of the scissors, carefully poke a hole in the center of this lower deck piece. Set aside.

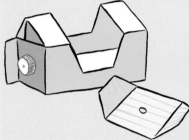

If necessary, pull open one side of the carton top as if you were going to drink from it. Cut off the triangular flaps on each side.

Cover the entire carton with masking tape, overlapping as you did with the lower deck piece. Repeat taping with a second layer, if needed, to fully cover the carton. This large piece will be the ship's hull.

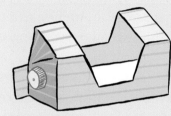

Stuff a small amount of newspaper into the hull. Place the lower deck (the cut piece) on top of the newspaper and press into place to make the bottom deck.

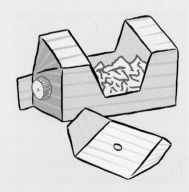

Cut a drinking straw to 4½ inches in length. Tape it to the front of the hull (the front of the ship) as shown.

With hole punch, punch a hole in each end of the top deck as shown.

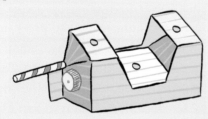

From a plastic grocery sack cut three squares, each measuring 5 by 5 inches, and one triangle, 6 inches tall and 4 inches wide (at the base), to use as the ship's sails. Tape the edges of the sails with masking tape as shown.

Tape one of the square sails to a drinking straw. Put two straws together, end to end, by pinching the end of one straw and sliding it into the open end of the other. Next, tape the other two square sails to this long straw, one above the other, leaving a small space between the two sails. Tape the triangular sail to another straw. Place the triangular sail/straw in the punched hole at the back of the ship. Tape in place from the bottom.

Place the taller straw with two sails in the hole in the center of the lower deck. Tape in place. Place the final sail/straw in the punched hole at the ship's front. Tape in place from the bottom.

Using scissors, cut small slits in the tops of each straw. Cut a length of string that is long enough to reach from the front straw and back through the slits in each of the other straws. Tie a knot in each end of the string. Carefully run the string through each mast (straw) slit.

Decorate the ship's sides with the colored markers, if desired.

* This design based on Spanish Galleon craft created by Mark Icanberry, www.looledo.com

21

EARTHQUAKE!

In July 1769, as the Portolá expedition camped near the Santa Ana River, they experienced an earthquake—and this was no ordinary quake. Using geological and historical records, researchers believe the earthquake Portolá and his men experienced may have been the largest earthquake in Los Angeles basin history. With an estimated magnitude of 7.3, this quake would have been even stronger than the 6.7 magnitude quake that occurred in Northridge in 1994.

A Colonization Expedition

In the late 1600s and early 1700s, Catholic priests worked to establish religious settlements called missions in Baja California. Spanish priests wanted to change the beliefs of Native Americans by converting them to the Catholic faith. Spanish officials thought they could turn California's Native Americans into Spanish citizens and use these newly converted natives to colonize the area for Spain.

Soon, Spanish officials decided to establish missions in Alta California as well. Spanish leaders believed this would be the best way to colonize the region. In 1768 Spanish official José de Gálvez (GAHL-vehs) began preparations for an expedition to settle Alta California.

Gálvez, along with New Spain governor Gaspar de Portolá (pohr-toh-LAH) and priest Junípero (hoo-NEE-peh-roh) Serra, planned and organized what would become known as the "Sacred Expedition." Both sea and land groups comprised the expedition. Those traveling by sea faced great hardship—one ship and its crew were lost at sea and scurvy devastated another.

The first land expedition, consisting mostly of soldiers, left Baja in March 1769. This group drove herds of cattle, horses, and mules northward. These animals would be necessary for the survival of the early mission settlers. In May, Father Serra, Captain Portolá, and another group of men began their overland journey.

While the land groups did not have the same difficulties as the sea expeditions, they faced hazards of their own. Rough terrain, gorges, desert and mountainous conditions, and other perils made travel dangerous. Serra, who chose to walk to Alta, was badly bothered by a leg infection, which was likely caused by either an insect or snake bite. At one point, Portolá tried to get Serra to turn back toward Baja.

But Serra was determined to press on—"Even though I should die on the way, I shall not turn back." Some reports estimate that only about half of the 300 men that attempted the journey by land or by sea actually made it to San Diego.

California Missions

The voyagers who survived the journey came together at San Diego on July 1, 1769. Sadly, the first jobs at the mission site were to care for the sailors sick with scurvy and to bury the dead. Even with the awful conditions at San Diego, Portolá decided to leave the group behind to continue on to Monterey.

While Portolá was away, Serra constructed a large cross and placed it near the San Diego River.

This would be the spot of Alta California's first mission: San Diego de Alcalá. The first mission building, temporarily located at the top of Presidio Hill, was rather simple, built with wooden stakes and a thatched roof. The first mission bells clanged to celebrate the event, as a passionate Serra readily blessed the setting.

The Sacred Expedition's first interactions with the Native Americans of the area occurred within its first few days in San Diego. Curious about Serra and his men, a few Native Americans made their way into the mission area. The men tried to talk with the natives, but since the groups spoke different languages, it was difficult, if not impossible, to communicate. The Spanish offered gifts such as food and clothing to the natives. The natives readily accepted the clothing, but

shunned the food; they saw the sickness within the camp and assumed it came from the food that the Spanish ate. Sadly, these first interactions in the mission system led to the eventual destruction of a large part of the native peoples and their way of life.

The Impact on Native Americans

Over a period of 54 years, Spanish priests established 21 missions along the California coastline, from San Diego to Sonoma. The missions covered nearly 10 million acres and were home to about two million cattle, horses, sheep, mules, and goats. Native Americans were forced, often under the threat of beatings, to keep the missions up and running.

(left) Mission San Diego, the first mission established in Alta California (1769).
Library of Congress, LC-DIG-ppmsca-18212

(right) Engraving of Native Americans dancing at California mission.
Library of Congress, LC-USZ62-116522

The natives were drawn into the missions when *padres* (priests) offered them clothing, glass beads, and other trinkets. When the native people became baptized, the priests called them neophytes. In the missions, neophytes learned about Christianity and learned trades, and some were introduced to the Spanish language. Men raised crops in fields or vineyards, or worked with livestock such as horses or cattle. Others worked as blacksmiths, brick makers, or leather workers. Women usually wove cloth or baskets or ground meal for cooking.

But sadly, mission life took its toll on the California Native American population. Many Indians suffered horribly at the missions. What the neophytes may not have originally known was that baptism bound them to the missions. Friars locked the neophytes in their rooms at night, and they were not allowed to leave the mission complex without permission. Some natives who hoped to return to their village homes ran away only to be caught and beaten for their disobedience. The native people also endured long workdays under the scorching sun, forced separation from their families, and brutal whippings when considered disobedient.

Europeans also brought with them diseases to which the native peoples had never been exposed. Smallpox, whooping cough, typhoid, measles, and other contagious illnesses sickened and killed many of the native peoples. Estimates show that about 300,000 Native Americans lived in California when the first settlers arrived. About one-third of those, or around 100,000, died as a consequence of European settlement. And not only did many Native Americans lose their lives; they lost their culture as well.

Spanish Mission Locations and Dates Established

Pacific Ocean

San Francisco Solano de Sonoma (1823)
San Rafael Arcangel (1817)
San Francisco de Asis (1776)
San Jose de Guadalupe (1797)
Santa Clara de Asis (1777)
Santa Cruz (1791)
San Juan Bautista (1797)
San Carlos Borromeo (1770)
Nuestra Senora de la Soledad (1791)
San Antonio de Padua (1771)
San Miguel Arcangel (1797)
San Luis Obispo de Tolosa (1772)
La Purisima Concepcion (1787)
Santa Ines (1804)
Santa Barbara (1786)
San Buenaventura (1782)
San Fernando Rey de Espana (1797)
San Gabriel Arcangel (1771)
San Juan Capistrano (1776)
San Luis Rey de Francia (1798)
San Diego de Alcala (1769)

"FATHER OF CALIFORNIA"

Junípero Serra remains an important but controversial part of California history. Considered by some as the Father of California, Serra was an interesting individual. A small man of just over five feet tall, Serra dedicated his life to sharing his Christian faith with others. Never one to back down from hardship, Serra walked thousands of miles during his lifetime in order to share God's word.

As did many priests, Serra also took a vow of poverty, which meant he lived with only the bare necessities. Serra slept on a bed made only of boards—with no mattress—and his few possessions included only one blanket, a candlestick, and a small amount of furniture. The only treatment he allowed to his ulcerated leg came from a mule driver. When Serra felt he could go no farther on his journey toward San Diego, he asked the muleteer traveling with the expedition to treat the injury as he would if it occurred on one of his mules. The muleteer applied a poultice of herbs and mud. Amazingly, the treatment relieved some of Serra's pain and allowed him to continue.

Many view Serra as a highly honorable man who devoted his life to helping others. In 1987 Pope John Paul II confirmed the second of three steps that would grant Serra sainthood, an honor bestowed on only a select few. Others, however, criticize this significant recognition for Serra. Many Native Americans feel that Serra and the entire mission system violated the religious and personal rights of native peoples through the beatings and harsh living conditions that ultimately contributed to the devastation of California's Native American population.

Statue of Junípero Serra (1713–84) by Ettore Cadorin located in the National Statuary Hall Collection, US Capitol, Washington, DC.
Architect of the Capitol

3

From Mexican California to an American Beginning

While Spain busied itself establishing missions in California, something else was going on in another part of North America. And that event would have a major impact on California's future. The people from the part of New Spain that is now Mexico were not happy under Spanish rule. They wanted to make their own decisions and govern themselves. They wanted their independence.

Early in the morning of September 16, 1810, in Dolores, Mexico, church bells rang out. People left their homes to hear what priest Father Miguel Hidalgo had to say. "My children . . . will you free yourselves?" he asked. "Will you recover the lands stolen 300 years ago from your forefathers by the hated Spaniards? We must act at once." Father Hidalgo wanted to remind the Mexican people that before being taken over by Spain, they lived the way they wanted. They made their own rules. Hidalgo's words led to a long and bloody battle that resulted in New Spain's independence from Spain 12 years later.

Californians had no idea about the war that raged in Mexico, which they knew as New Spain. In fact, they didn't find out that

Mexican Californians enjoying a musical serenade.
Library of Congress, LC-DIG-ppmsca-02888

Mexico had gained its independence until almost a year after the war had ended in 1821. But with Mexico's victory, both Baja and Alta California became Mexican territories. Over time, this fact significantly changed life in California.

Secularization of the Missions

During California's mission period, the Spanish wanted to transform the native peoples into "civilized" Spanish citizens. Spanish officials believed that colonizing the area with these "new" citizens would secure the region for Spain.

Spain, however, did not expect the missions to last forever. Spanish officials believed that within 10 to 20 years of mission life, the neophytes would be able to support themselves through what they'd learned in the missions. Once this goal was reached, the Native Americans were to be given a portion of the mission lands. Unfortunately for the native people, this never truly occurred.

Diseño of Rancho Cienga o Paso de la Tijera (ca. 1852). *National Archives, ARC ID 595794*

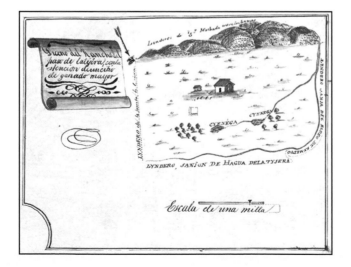

With Mexico's independence, the idea of secularization—the dissolving of the mission system—grew even more important because the Mexican people knew how it felt to be treated poorly and unequally. In 1834 California's Mexican territorial governor, José Figueroa, proclaimed the missions would be closed. He also declared that one half of the mission land and properties would be distributed to the mission natives.

Sadly, Figueroa died the following year, and California's mission natives saw very little of the mission properties. Instead of giving the native people their share of livestock, land, and other properties, officials often sold or gave them away to new Mexican settlers or to important Californios, the original Spanish colonists who had settled in California.

Californios and Ranchos

Governors that came after Figueroa distributed mission lands to around 700 people. In order to request a parcel of land, people drew up simple maps called *diseños* (dee-SAYN-yos). These hand-drawn maps were very basic and often used groves of trees, hills, rock formations, streams, and other landmarks to denote the property's boundaries. Some mapmakers worked from horseback. As they rode the property's intended boundaries, they stretched out lengths of rope on the ground and counted the number of rope-lengths it took to get from one corner to another. Since they didn't have survey equipment or measuring tapes, this was the only way they had to include measurements on their maps.

DRAW YOUR OWN DISEÑO

Map out an area in the same way Californios and Mexican settlers did in the 1830s.

Materials

Notebook for sketching

Pencil

Helper

Rope (25 feet is a good length)

Large brown paper bag

Scissors

Colored markers or crayons

☞ Find an area around your home, school, or park that you would like to map as your rancho. Sketch out the approximate shape of the area. Beginning at the front left corner, have your helper hold one end of the rope while you extend it down the boundary line to the back left corner of your area. This marks one rope-length.

Your helper then comes to where you are standing and you again stretch the rope down the boundary. When the rope is fully stretched, this will be your second rope-length. Continue stretching the rope down the boundary line and counting the rope-lengths until you reach the back left corner. In some instances, you may have to estimate by using half rope-lengths, such as "4½ rope lengths."

Write down the number of rope-lengths for each side on your sketch.

Repeat this process for all sides of your rancho area. Remember, your area does not have to be a perfect square or rectangle.

With your sketchbook and pencil, draw out the physical features of the land. Note any large trees or tree groupings, any rock clusters, any streams, hills, or ditches. Draw anything that will help someone picture the area you are mapping. When these steps are complete, you are ready to draw your *diseño*.

Cut out a large section from the paper bag and use your markers or crayons to draw the shape of your rancho. Write in the rope-lengths of each side. Next, draw the physical features of the land that you sketched. Finally, give your rancho a name and write it at the top. To make the map look aged, you can crumple it slightly, then flatten it back out.

Official regulations stated that individuals could receive a maximum of 50,000 acres of land, but some received more simply because they applied for a grant for each family member. Surprisingly, in an era when women had few rights, about 60 women were awarded land grants. The Californios' and Mexican settlers' ownership of these huge tracts of land, called ranchos, gave their owners great power within the region.

Some Native Americans received small portions of land, but few, if any, made livings from their plots. Many natives did not even know that part of the mission land was rightfully theirs. After the decline of the missions, many native people went to work for Californios at established ranchos.

Life on a rancho was often harsh for the Native Americans. Women cleaned the homes of the rancheros (ranch owners), looked after their children, sewed clothing, and cooked meals. Men worked long hours in fields or as horsemen

or cattle wranglers, who were sometimes called vaqueros, California's first cowboys. The native people received little or no money for their work. They instead received shelter, food, and clothing as pay.

Cattle grazed on millions of acres of rancho land throughout California. Although beef was important, rancheros made their livings mostly by trading the cowhides and tallow the cattle provided. Tallow, the fat from the cattle, was used to make soap and candles. In order to make tallow, native laborers scraped fat from the cowhides and boiled it in giant kettles. After the tallow cooled, it was poured into large cowhide bags called *botas* so it could be sold.

Since California had a trade, or barter, economy, Californios did not use coins or paper money. Instead, they considered the cowhides, which they sometimes called "California banknotes," their currency. As visitors sailed to California from Boston and other areas, they brought such items as clothing, furniture, jewelry, shoes, tools, spices, and even toothbrushes to trade for the rancheros' hides and tallow. The visitors returned home with tallow for soaps and candles and with hides that could be used to make leather goods such as shoes and saddles.

Many of the wealthiest rancheros lived carefree lives. The native peoples performed the majority of the work on their immense ranchos, giving the rancheros plenty of time to enjoy themselves. Huge fiestas, weddings, rodeos, and other celebrations often occurred, sometimes lasting up to a week. Guests danced to upbeat violin and

Vaqueros roping a bull.
Library of Congress,
LC-USZ62-48135

DESIGN YOUR OWN BRAND

Many Mexican rancheros owned thousands of head of cattle. Fences did not surround the huge ranchos, so rancheros had to have a way to determine which cattle belonged to them. To do this, they used brands. The brands they designed often used letters, numbers, or symbols.

Rancheros often included their initials in their brands. Look at the images here—if a letter rests on its "back," when reading the brand, you put "lazy" in front of the letter. If a — precedes, follows, or is above or below a letter or number, the brand is read left to right (or top to bottom) using the word "bar." You can also see how circles, diamonds, and "rocking" symbols are used and read.

LAZY E RANCH

KS RANCH

ROCKING L RANCH

BD RANCH

BAR J RANCH

DIAMOND D RANCH

BAR RD RANCH

HMT RANCH

Now it's time to design your own brand.

Materials

Pencil

Paper

Small blank stickers (circles, squares, ovals, rectangles, etc.)

Colored markers

☞ Begin by sketching on paper some ideas you might like to use for your brand. Experiment with different letters, numbers, and symbols. You may wish to include your initials, your age, or something else that's important to you.

When you've decided on your perfect brand, draw it lightly onto the stickers. Using the colored markers, trace over your design—you may want to use two or more colors to draw your brand.

Once done, use these stickers to "brand" your property—notebooks, lunch bag, skateboard, backpack, and more.

Trapper searching for game.
Library of Congress, LC-USZ62-2034

guitar music, the clapping of hands, and the click of castanets, and enjoyed huge feasts topped off by tasty cakes and pastries.

At some fiestas, guests broke cologne-filled eggs, sometimes called *cascarones*, over each other's heads. Elegantly dressed women would sneak up behind a man, yank off his sombrero, crack the egg atop his head, and then race off before being seen. It was then the man's job to discover the woman who had "egged" him so he could return the favor.

Another fascinating, yet more gruesome, pastime also took place at some fiestas or rodeos—bull-and-bear fights. A captured California grizzly bear and one of the rancho's bulls were placed in a bullring. A brave vacquero would then chain one of the bear's hind legs to a front leg of the bull, and the fight would begin. Spectators placed bets on whether the bull or the bear would be the last animal standing.

Visitors from the Eastern United States

As rancheros kicked up their heels at fiestas, change was coming to California. People from other parts of the United States began taking greater notice of the isolated California territory.

Some of the first American pioneers that came to the area were trappers. American trappers realized a market existed for valuable beaver, sea otter, and other furs. Sea otter pelts could be sold in China for about $300 each, an enormous amount of money in those days. Since an abundance of these animals could be found in California's wilderness and along its coast, it made sense that trappers would travel there to hunt. These early trappers may not have realized how important their overland trails would be in California's future.

Jedediah Smith

In 1826 Jedediah Smith, a strapping 27-year-old who stood six foot three, led a group of beaver trappers west. Trappers had killed so many beaver in the eastern United States that there were hardly any left. Smith and his men knew the sparsely populated land in the west had been hunted very little. Smith's group traveled over land that others had never crossed. They blazed new trails from Utah through the Mojave Desert and on to the San Diego area.

The Smith Party became the first recorded overland expedition to California and the first white men known to have crossed the Sierra Nevada range. Their journey wasn't easy. They faced attacks from Native Americans, lack of water, and near starvation as they crossed both the Mojave Desert and the Sierra Nevada. Smith was even arrested when Mexican officials accused him of being a spy. At one point, the group had to kill one of their travel-weary horses in order to have food to eat. Smith wrote, "It was bad eating, but we were hungry enough to eat anything."

Smith's accomplishments are sometimes overlooked, but they are noteworthy because the trails he blazed allowed others to follow in his footsteps.

Early American Settlers

Since Mexico controlled the California territory, Mexican officials were not happy about Americans and others coming into the region. They worried that the area could be taken over by these "foreigners." In fact, before a person could enter the territory, he or she had to obtain official permission or a passport. Imagine needing a passport to enter California! Anyone who showed up without one, as Jedediah Smith learned, could be arrested or jailed.

As more and more traders and trappers visited California, interest in the territory rose. Letters and reports sent back from the West included

BEAR!

Mountain men like Jedediah Smith were known for their toughness. They often trekked on horseback for miles and miles each day across uncharted territory in all types of weather. Smith knew firsthand the dangers of animal encounters along the trail.

In 1823, while Smith was hunting in the Rockies, a grizzly bear emerged from the brush and mauled Smith. The grizzly's jaws wrapped around Smith's head, and the bear slung him to the ground, breaking several ribs. Smith's scalp was almost completely ripped off and one ear dangled from the side of his head. Miraculously, Smith remained alert during the ordeal and afterward.

After what seemed like hours, the bear bolted back into the woods. Smith looked to one of his men, James Clyman, to dress his wounds. Clyman found a needle and thread and went to work on Smith's scalp. When he looked at the ear, however, Clyman told Smith he didn't think there was anything he could do for it. Smith insisted that Clyman "stick [it] up some way or other." Clyman wrote in his journal, "I put my needle sticking it through and through and over and over laying the lacerated parts together as nice as I could with my hands."

The attack would leave Smith scarred for life, but tough mountain men never quit. In less than two weeks Smith was back leading his group.

Emigrant wagon train in Strawberry Valley, California.
Library of Congress, LC-USZC4-4580

glowing reviews of the climate and fertile land. When people from the East daydreamed about the vast territory, they became excited. Could wealth and opportunity be only a wagon-train ride away?

Eventually, people from such places as Independence, Missouri; Council Bluffs, Iowa; Santa Fe, New Mexico; and elsewhere loaded provisions onto wagons. Coffee, lard, beans, salt, bacon, and flour were piled atop the wagons, as were candles, clothing, soap, hunting guns, and tools. Supplies had to be loaded carefully for travel over rough terrain; if the wagons became unbalanced, they could easily overturn. When preparations were complete, the pioneers hitched up teams of mule or oxen, tugged on their most reliable walking shoes, and headed west.

Bartleson-Bidwell Party

In 1841, a group known as the Bartleson-Bidwell Party, members of the Western Migration Society, set out on their adventure to California. The group of 69 men, women, and children left their jumping-off point of Sapling Grove, Missouri, in May 1841. One party member, Nancy Kelsey, had a very special kind of cargo—she planned on carrying her infant daughter the entire way. When asked why she decided to join the difficult (if not impossible) journey, Nancy stated simply, "Where my husband can go, I can go."

The group had little in the way of accurately drawn maps to lead them, and none had ever traveled west before. John Bidwell, a former schoolteacher and one of the party's organizers, realized the difficulty of the group's endeavor—"Our ignorance of the route was complete. We knew that California lay west, and that was the extent of our knowledge." Before they made their way down the Oregon Trail through present-day Kansas, Nebraska, Wyoming, and Idaho, the party connected with a mountain man named Thomas "Broken Hand" Fitzpatrick who assisted them in their travels.

When it came time to leave the established trail, some of the party members began to have second thoughts. They had faced days and nights of Native American encounters, thirst and hunger, and storms with hail "as large as turkey's eggs." About half of the emigrants headed on, but some were so discouraged that they turned back toward their Missouri homes. The remaining group, with their nine wagons, continued on "with no guide, no compass, nothing but the sun to direct them."

Travel, difficult from the beginning, became extremely grueling in northeastern Nevada, and the Bartleson-Bidwell Party was forced to abandon their wagons: "Let us leave our wagons, otherwise the snows will overtake us before we get to California."

They packed whatever possible in pack saddles and strapped them to the backs of the oxen, horses, and mules; anything that couldn't fit was abandoned. The fearless group pressed on, however, and made their way over the Sierra Nevada. They arrived half starved in northern California in November 1841, about seven months after leaving Missouri. The group's 2,500-mile trek proved that, although not easy, overland travel was possible.

By the early 1840s, around 2,500 Americans had endured rugged journeys to settle in California. Some of the settlers that came west became Mexican citizens. Others, however, settled there illegally. Considered "squatters," these settlers simply arrived in California, found desirable pieces of ground, and established homes there; they did not rightfully own the property on which they lived.

As more and more American settlers staked out pieces of land, the Californios became restless. They weren't sure they wanted these outsiders

THE DONNER PARTY

The James Frazier Reed family and the George and Jacob Donner families had heard the stories of health and fortune that were rumored to be found in California. They wanted to see for themselves if what was written about California was true. Was it truly a place of "fertile and productive [soil], . . . a climate of mildness, . . . [and a place that would] promote unbounded happiness and prosperity"?

In mid-May 1846, the 87 men, women, and children that comprised the Donner Party headed west from Independence, Missouri. Heavy spring rains caused the group to fall somewhat behind schedule, so instead of taking the established route, the party decided to follow a "shortcut" called Hastings Cutoff. Unfortunately, taking the "shortcut" was a deadly decision. The route ended up being about 125 miles longer and much more treacherous than the established trail.

With winter rapidly approaching, the group knew they would have to hurry if they wanted to make it across the mountains before snow blocked their way. The day before they planned on tackling the Sierra Nevada summit, a massive snowstorm hit. Twenty-foot snowdrifts shut down further attempts to cross the mountains, forcing the group to camp in the foothills.

Out of food, the groups ate whatever they could find—bark, cattle hide, bones, twigs, leaves. Starvation began to take its toll. Those that were alive had no choice—some sources report that they began to eat the flesh of the dead in order to save themselves.

When help arrived, only 46 of the 87 people who set out with the Donner Party from Missouri almost a year earlier had lived through the winter. The route the Donner Party traveled later became known as Donner Pass.

Survivor Virginia Reed, stepdaughter of James Reed, summed up the ordeal in a letter with this advice to her sister: "Never take no shortcuts and hurry along as fast as you can."

invading their region—especially if they were not willing to follow the Californios' rules. And since American settlers didn't like being under Mexican control, tensions in California mounted. Due to the fact that the California territory was so isolated and difficult to reach, it was almost impossible for the Mexican government to control the events taking place there.

About this time, people in the eastern part of the United States began to think seriously about the California region. They talked about a concept called Manifest Destiny. Manifest Destiny supporters thought it was not only the duty of the American people, but also God's will, to move westward in order to extend the US borders from the Atlantic Ocean in the east to the Pacific Ocean in the west. The slogan "Go west, young man," promoted by American journalists and politicians, ignited the desire to make America a truly continental nation.

John Charles Frémont and the Bear Flag Revolt

In 1845, US Army captain John C. Frémont arrived in California with 60 men. Supposedly on a mission to explore the Sierra Nevada trails used by overland emigrants, Frémont had other ideas circulating in his mind. He wanted to secure the California territory for the United States and in turn make a name for himself.

Mexican officials weren't happy to see Frémont back for his third visit to California. They saw trouble ahead, and they were right. In spring 1846, Frémont heard that a group of Americans near Sonoma had planned a revolt against the Californios. Frémont and his men joined forces with the revolt group and declared themselves an independent republic. To symbolize the act, the men created a flag that depicted drawings of a bear and a star along with the words "California Republic." The "bear flag" had been born.

Frémont's group made their way across the San Francisco Bay and easily destroyed the decrepit Spanish canons at the rundown San Francisco presidio (military fort). For the most part, Frémont's actions were merely for show. Many believe Frémont wanted to run for president of

Portrait of John Charles Frémont (1813–90).
Library of Congress, LC-DIG-pga-00431

the United States in the future, so he participated in the revolt in order to be seen as a national hero.

Frémont's Bear Republic didn't last long, however. About a month after they raised the bear flag over Sonoma, Frémont's forces learned that war had officially been declared between Mexico and the United States. The first American battleships entered Monterey harbor. Even though Frémont had not officially been sent by the government to bring about war, his actions played a key role in raising tensions between the Americans and the Californios.

At War with Mexico

Bitter feelings existed between the United States and Mexico partly because the United States had taken possession of Mexican-controlled Texas in December 1845. Mexico hinted at war at that time, but Mexican officials hesitated because they knew they would be in for a major fight.

At the same time, the United States had concerns about Britain. If Britain learned of the unrest in California, it might try to take advantage of the situation by sending its own ships to the area. With the already present friction with Mexico, the threat from Britain, and the concept of Manifest Destiny firmly in mind, the United States declared war on Mexico.

The United States made quick work of the early days of the war. American forces swiftly took Monterey, as the Mexicans there put up little resistance. Officials celebrated by raising the American flag over the city. Only days later, the US flag also flew over Yerba Buena (present-day

THE BEAR FLAG

William L. Todd is believed to have been the creator of the original bear flag that was hoisted over Sonoma in 1846. The flag itself was made from a piece of cotton material. Red flannel, possibly from an old flannel shirt, was used for a stripe along the bottom. The words "California Republic," a star, and a grizzly bear were either painted with linseed oil paints or stained with "lamp-black and poke-berries." According to one report, when the finished flag was raised, nearby Mexicans shouted, "Cochino!"—or "little hog." Apparently, many thought Todd's grizzly bear looked more like a pig!

San Francisco). San Diego and then Los Angeles were soon overtaken. Many Americans believed the war was over before it had even begun. But that was not completely the case. Some Californios were not quite ready to give up their fight.

Californio revolts took place in various parts of California, sometimes temporarily taking back territory claimed by the United States. One notable uprising occurred at the Battle of Pasqual, a confrontation some consider the bloodiest battle of the war. US forces, learning of a rebel group stationed near San Pasqual, crept into a foggy darkness to try to steal the Californios' horses. When the Americans clashed with the Californios, they met strong resistance from the Californios' razor-sharp, 20-foot-long lances. Twenty-two Americans died in the battle with 16 more injured.

Californio revolts proved to be a setback for the Americans, but the Californios did not have the final word. On January 13, 1847, Mexican officials surrendered to the Americans through the Capitulation of Cahuenga.

The war between Mexico and the United States was not declared officially over until the signing of the Treaty of Guadalupe Hildalgo on February 2, 1848. Under the treaty's terms, Mexico surrendered almost one-half of all its territory, including New Mexico, Arizona, Utah, Nevada, and California, along with parts of other states, to the United States in exchange for $15 million. The Americans' dream of a continental nation, of its Manifest Destiny, was being realized.

ACTIVITY ▶

WAVE YOUR FLAG

Just as John Frémont and his group created a flag to commemorate California's Bear Flag Republic, you can make your own special flag to honor your city, state, school, country, or even your room. What makes these places special? Use your ideas to design your own flag.

Adult supervision required

Materials

Standard-sized pillowcase
Scissors
Cardboard
Pencil
Paper
Decorative items such as fabric paint, iron-on letters/decorations, puff paint, glitter, felt, ribbon, etc.
Glue
½-inch-diameter wooden dowel rod
Hot glue gun
Hot glue sticks
Old towel

☞ If you're using a new pillowcase, wash and dry it first to remove wrinkles and to make sure that paint will adhere. Use scissors to cut a piece of cardboard that is a little smaller than the pillowcase. Slide the cardboard into the pillowcase. This will make painting and decorating your flag much easier.

Sketch out some ideas on paper, and then decide on your design. Leaving the pillowcase opening on the left side, sketch your design on the pillowcase lightly with the pencil. Lay out other decorative items. If you are including iron-ons, ask an adult to help you iron them onto the pillowcase, but *remove the cardboard before ironing*. With the cardboard in place, glue on felt pieces, ribbon, glitter, or other decorative materials, if desired. Then use fabric or puff paints to paint your design. Let it dry completely.

To attach your flagpole, place one end of the dowel rod down the left-hand side of your flag a few inches from the edge. With the rod in place, use the hot glue gun to run glue down the side and top of the rod. Fold the end of the pillowcase over the rod, cover the fabric with an old towel to avoid contact with the hot glue, and carefully press down on the fabric until it sticks to the pole. Hot glue the "flap" of leftover material down onto your flag, and then use a little hot glue to close up the opening of the pillowcase.

Proudly display your flag (indoors only).

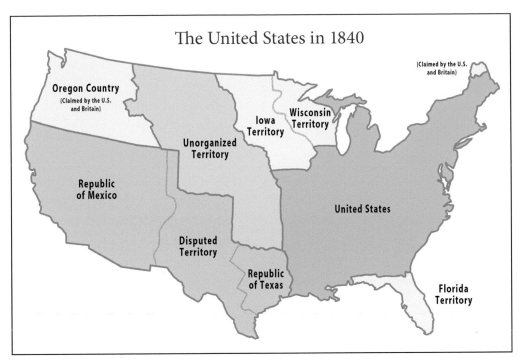

The United States in 1840

Oregon Country
(Claimed by the U.S. and Britain)

(Claimed by the U.S. and Britain)

Wisconsin Territory

Iowa Territory

Unorganized Territory

Republic of Mexico

United States

Disputed Territory

Republic of Texas

Florida Territory

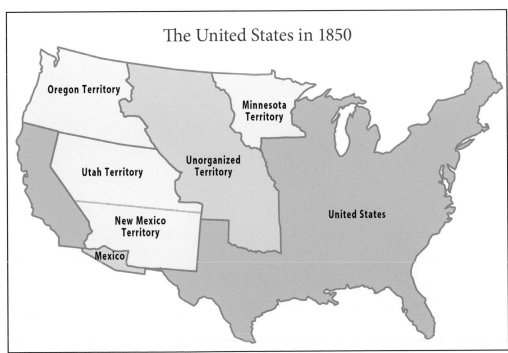

The United States in 1850

Oregon Territory

Minnesota Territory

Utah Territory

Unorganized Territory

New Mexico Territory

United States

Mexico

4

Gold! and Statehood

When John Frémont and other Americans fought to seize control of California from Mexico, they had no idea what the future held for this new territory. Only nine days before Mexican and American officials signed the Treaty of Guadalupe Hildalgo, an event that would forever rock California, the United States, and perhaps even the world, took place on the south fork of the American River: the discovery of gold.

In 1848, California, still a fairly isolated region, was home to only about 14,000 non-Native Americans. After news of the gold discovery spread, California's population grew not by thousands, but by hundreds of thousands.

James Marshall and Sutter's Mill

In early 1848, carpenter James Marshall oversaw work on a saw-mill in the ponderosa pine–covered foothills of the Sierra Nevada. Businessman John A. Sutter had hired Marshall to build the mill near present-day Coloma, a place the Miwoks called *cullumah*, which means "beautiful vale or valley." Sutter wanted to mill lumber to sell to others and for his own building projects in Yerba Buena (present-day San Francisco).

One chilly January morning, Marshall went to check the progress of the mill. As he inspected the river channel that would carry water away from the mill, Marshall noticed a glimmer. "My eye

A view of the American River at Rattlesnake Bar, the river where gold was first found.
Library of Congress, LC-USZ62-26938

fortis," a type of nitric acid. The conclusion: gold. Genuine gold.

Marshall and Sutter decided to keep the news quiet, at least until the mill was completed. They knew if word of the discovery got out it would be impossible to get the mill into operation. Many of the workers knew of the find, and of course they wanted to search for gold as well, but to keep the mill project on schedule Sutter convinced them to only prospect during nonworking hours.

But keeping the secret would prove impossible. Little by little, word of gold on the American River leaked out, and then one day, it seemed as if *everyone* knew.

Sam Brannan and the Early Days

Like many others, Sam Brannan, a local general store owner, had heard stories of the gold discovery, but he didn't put much stock in them. His mind changed, however, when some of Sutter's men paid for goods at Brannan's store with gold nuggets. The rumors might indeed be true. As a businessman, Brannan knew the discovery of gold would be good for his business. People would flock to the area, and they would certainly need to buy items he stocked, such as picks, shovels, pans, tents, blankets, buckets, and food. So Brannan did what he had to do: he headed to San Francisco with a small bottle filled with gold. To stir up enthusiasm, he raced through the city's streets, waved the bottle in the air, and shouted "Gold! Gold! Gold!"

Brannan's outburst unleashed a gold frenzy. Could a fortune in gold really be found only

was caught by something shining in the bottom of the ditch. . . . I reached my hand down and picked it up; it made my heart thump, for I was certain it was gold."

To ensure what he'd found was real gold, Marshall bent a flake with his fingernail, then pounded it with a rock. One of his workers took a nugget to his wife to boil in lye soap; lye can corrode some metals, but not gold. The American River nugget remained intact.

When Marshall felt confident that what he'd found was truly gold, he rode to Sutter's Fort to show his employer. Sutter was intrigued but not totally convinced. He pulled the *Encyclopedia Americana* from his shelf and looked up "gold" to determine the best testing methods. The men performed another test—this time with "aqua miles from their homes? Were riches only a pan and pickax away?

It took some time for the initial gold rush to come into full swing, but by spring of 1848, many people left their homes and jobs to follow their dreams of untold wealth. According to Monterey's mayor, Walter Colton, "The blacksmith dropped his hammer, the carpenter his plane, the mason his trowel, the farmer his sickle, the baker his loaf." Military men left their posts behind; newspapers closed with no workers to staff them; farmers left fields half planted. Some reports noted that perhaps three-quarters of San Franciscan men fled the town, leaving it nearly empty. It seemed almost every Californian from San Jose to Los Angeles, Monterey to San Diego, and all areas in between wanted to be a part of the fledgling gold rush. And that was just the beginning.

By the middle of 1848, news had indeed spread, but with no telephones, telegraphs, or cross-country railroads, it took time for the news to reach the East Coast. But that was soon to change as well. A military officer sent a report of the discovery to President James K. Polk, and he sent along some proof, too—230 ounces of gold packed into a tin.

The news reached the president late in the year, and by December 5, 1848, he announced his findings: "The accounts of the abundance of gold in that territory are of such extraordinary character as would scarcely command belief were they not corroborated by authentic reports of officers in the public service." Polk's words and dozens of newspaper reports of the discovery caused excitement to grow. People the world over were struck with gold fever.

By 1849, the news of gold in California was widespread. With dreams of riches in their heads, people traveled to California from such places as Peru, Australia, Mexico, Europe, China, and other countries. All told, nearly 100,000 gold seekers converged on California in 1849. Most of those who arrived came from the United States, and many of those first forty-niners arrived by ship.

By Sea or Over Land

Some potential prospectors traveled established sea-trade routes from places such as China and Hawaii. Others, however, including those traveling by sea from the eastern United States, faced a much more difficult sea voyage. An ocean trip from the East Coast covered 18,000 miles and took five to eight months or more if the voyager sailed down the eastern coast of South America, around Cape Horn, and back northward to California.

An alternative route allowed travelers to take a shortcut through Panama. Although the shortcut significantly shortened voyage time, it was considered dangerous. Once at the town of Chagres, Panama, travelers disembarked from the ship, natives rowed them up the Chagres River, and then they walked or rode mules on a two- to three-day trek through the jungle. The risky journey exposed travelers to such ills as robbery, violence, accident, illness, drowning, or alligator attack. Once they arrived on the Pacific side of

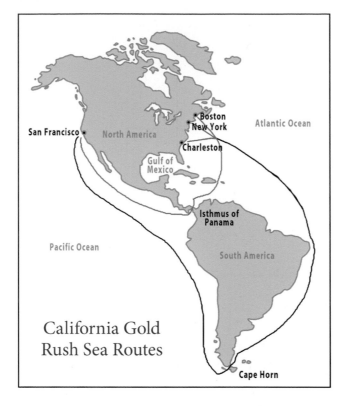

California Gold Rush Sea Routes

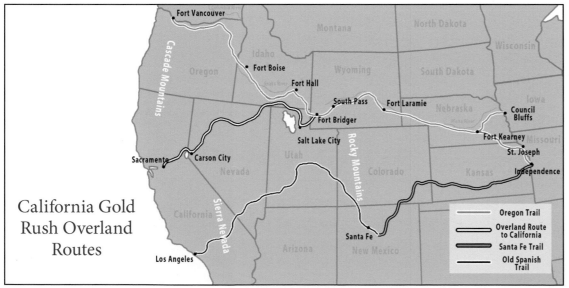

California Gold Rush Overland Routes

Panama, they then boarded another vessel for the final voyage to California. In the early days, one major downfall of the shortcut was the time it took to be able to board a ship northward to California. People often had to wait for weeks or even months in Panama before being admitted onto a vessel bound for gold country.

Many eager miners wanted to be the first to steam to California. They feared that if they did not arrive early, all the gold would be gone before they arrived. Unfortunately for these anxious miners, regularly scheduled passenger service to San Francisco did not exist at the beginning of the gold rush. People simply had to wait. But there were some who could afford *not* to wait; these passengers paid more than $1,000 to be the first on board one of the California-bound steamers.

While many gold seekers traveled by sea, the majority of those from the eastern and midwestern United States traveled by land via the Oregon-California Trail. In their excitement, many migrants were not properly prepared as they rushed off to the trails.

Timing for departures was critical. If travelers left too early in the year, their oxen would have little if any grass on which to graze. But if they left too late, they might become entrapped in snows in the Sierra Nevada—the fate that had befallen the Donner Party in 1846.

Just as with the travels of the Bartleson and Donner parties, difficulties plagued emigrants on the trails west. Over time, however, the miles-long wagon trains that traversed the routes helped the trails became more established and somewhat more easily traveled.

On good days, emigrants hoped to travel 18 to 20 miles. But the broken-in trails didn't mean life on the trail was without its hardships. Overland emigrants still had to deal with flooded rivers, poor weather, deserts, mountain crossings, hunger, thirst, and illness. Drownings in swollen rivers took the lives of many travelers. Others died from accidental gunshots or after falling from and being run over by wagons.

Along with these difficulties, a deadly illness also became particularly prevalent—cholera. Unsanitary living conditions along the trail spread the illness by tainting food and water sources and caused the disease to evolve into an epidemic. One emigrant, William Swain, wrote in a letter, "Today is still damp and gloomy, the

CROSSING THE ISTHMUS OF PANAMA

In a letter written in May 1849, Mary Jane Megquier recounts her travel across Panama: "[W]e were stored in a canoe . . . twenty feet long two feet wide with all our luggage which brought the top of the canoe very near the waters edge. . . . Every few miles . . . you can get a cup of miserable muddy coffee with hard bread of which we made dinner . . . [and ate] under a broiling sun the thermometer at one hundred. [We later] resumed our journey . . . on the backs of the most miserable apologies for horseflesh . . . over one of the roughest roads in the world, nothing but a path wide enough for the feet of the mule, which if he should make a mistake you would go to parts unknown."

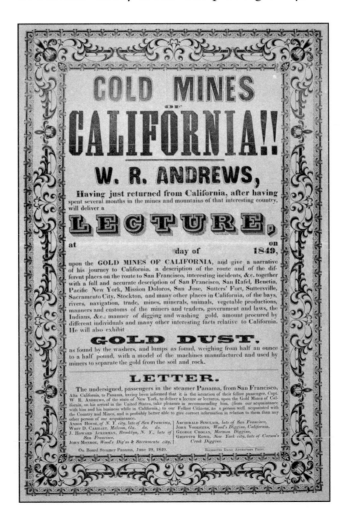

Poster promoting a lecture about the adventures of gold mining. *Library of Congress, Printed Ephemera Collection, Portfolio 120, 24d*

As thousands of gold seekers made their way to California by land and by sea, one industrious inventor thought about an interesting new route—by air! One day while taking a walk, Rufus Porter began thinking about alternate ways to travel. In 1849, Porter published a booklet that outlined his Aerial Locomotive, an aerial ship that could provide "pleasant and safe" travel "from New-York to California in three days." Porter expected his 800-foot-long, hydrogen-filled ship to travel at speeds of 60 to 100 miles per hour and carry 50 to 100 passengers. Porter gave demonstrations of a small version of his airship in New York in 1848 and 1849, but people didn't believe his full-sized version could ever be used to transport gold seekers—and they were right. I guess you could say Porter's idea never fully got off the ground.

weather being foggy. The cholera is still raging, and gloom appears on the countenances of all persons." Sadly, the travelers didn't realize how the disease was being spread, or know the proper way to treat it, and many died.

In looking at all causes of death on the trail, estimates note that about 1 in 10 people who set out overland died before making it to California.

The Mines

For those who did make it to California, a new adventure awaited them. Bearing names such as Poppysquash Hill, Grizzly Flat, Little Humbug Creek, Devil's Retreat, and Poverty Hill, camps sprung up far and wide in the Sierra Nevada foothills. Those who had survived their arduous journeys gathered shovels, picks, pans, and other supplies. They hoped to immediately strike it rich. Miners first located a suitable area and "staked a claim" as a way to show that the area belonged to them. Then they went to work.

Miners soon learned that finding gold wasn't as easy as simply picking it up from the ground, as James Marshall had done. Many of the early miners used a panning method to find gold. When panning, miners first used picks, shovels, and even knives, to dig out material from crevices, ditches, and rock outcroppings. They then scooped up a pan full of the material, filled the pan with river water, and then carefully swirled around the contents in a circular motion. In this manner, dirt, sand, and other particles would be sifted out and the heavier gold would be left behind. This method might seem easy, but it was far from it. Miners spent hours digging, bending, and squatting in scorching heat or in icy water.

Soon, anxious miners began to look for better, more productive ways to mine. The wooden rocker or cradle was an early answer. With this method, miners could process much more material at one time than they could with pans. Workers first shoveled dirt into a box on top of the

BAKE A HARDTACK SNACK

While at work in the mines, forty-niners had to eat whatever they had on hand. One of their main provisions was a cracker-like biscuit called hardtack. Its inexpensive ingredients, long shelf life, and the fact that it wouldn't easily crumble in bags or pockets made it suitable food for mine work.

Here's a recipe so you can bake your own batch. But beware! It lives up to its nicknames—"tooth dullers" and "sheet iron crackers"!

Adult supervision required

Materials

2 cups all-purpose flour
¾ teaspoon salt
1 tablespoon shortening
¾ cup water
Mixing bowl
Baking sheet
Large mixing spoon
Knife or pizza cutter
Fork
Spatula

☛ Wash your hands before beginning. Preheat your oven to 400°F. Mix flour and salt in the mixing bowl. Add shortening. Use the back of the large spoon to mix and press the shortening into the flour. It may take a few minutes to mix in the shortening.

Next, add water to the flour mixture. Stir well. In order to combine thoroughly, you will have to use your hands to complete the mixing. Form the mixture into a ball.

Press the dough onto an ungreased baking sheet to about a ½-inch thickness. (The dough will not cover the entire baking sheet.) With help from an adult, use a knife or pizza cutter to cut the dough into 2- to 3-inch squares. Use the fork tines to poke four rows of holes into the dough.

Bake at 400°F for 20 to 25 minutes. With adult assistance, remove the baking sheet from the oven and flip the hardtack over with a spatula. Return it to the oven and bake 20 to 25 minutes more.

Remove from the oven. Let cool completely before eating.

You can tough it out and eat hardtack plain, just like the forty-niners, or you may want to add a little peanut butter or jelly to make it tastier. Remember, hardtack is *hard*. Some miners soaked it in coffee to soften it up first. Be careful when eating it!

Miner using a rocker in Columbia, Tuloumne County.
Library of Congress, LC-USZ62-13127

rocker. Then, while one miner poured water onto the material, another shifted the rocker back and forth, something like rocking a cradle. The water flushed away dirt and other particles through small holes on the bottom of the box. Then, if the miner was lucky, gold pieces would be found left behind in the box on the rocker's lower end.

Prospectors kept looking for ways to increase production; the more material they could sift through, the more gold they might be able to find. As an extension of the rocker, miners developed a contraption called a long tom. It took about six to eight men to properly run the 12- to 15-foot-long device that worked similar to the rocker but processed material much more quickly.

As the gold rush continued, it became more and more difficult for miners to find gold using panning and rocker techniques. Much of the gold that rested close to the top of the ground had been mined. But gold remained deep underground in quartz deposits. Getting to this hidden treasure eluded most individual prospectors. They simply did not have the resources to bring in the equipment needed to dig up the gold.

The owners of large businesses, however, realized they could invest in new mining methods and could expect to make a great deal of money in return. During the mid to late 1800s, mining companies employed hydraulic mining to reach the previously untouchable gold. With hydraulic mining, miners used high-pressure hoses or pipes to blast streams of water against hillsides and riverbanks to separate the gold from the surrounding dirt and rock.

DESTRUCTION OF THE LAND

Hydraulic mining devastated areas of California's environment. Hydraulic miners often added mercury, a type of liquid metal, to their wash troughs. The addition of mercury made it easier for miners to separate and trap the gold particles. Unfortunately, this mercury contaminated water and soil and was harmful to plants and animals. Additionally, the hydraulic mining process washed tons of sand, soil, rock, and other material from hillsides and ridge tops onto low-lying towns below. This debris also filled river channels, a process that caused severe flooding in areas downstream from the mines. In several cases, mining wastes destroyed entire farms.

Eight-foot-high silt deposits became commonplace in Sacramento and other areas, and at one point, so much sand and debris filled the Sacramento River channel that boats could barely make their way down it.

By the late 1880s the people of the Central Valley had had enough. It wasn't easy, but they fought the mining companies and eventually won. The Sawyer Decision of 1884 led to the banning of hydraulic mining. To view hydraulic mining's effects firsthand, visit Malakoff Diggins State Historic Park (www.parks.ca.gov/default.asp?page_id=494) in Nevada County, California.

Hydraulic mining in Nevada County demonstrates the destruction created by the force of the water.
Library of Congress, LC-USZ62-9889

CREATE AND SEND A LETTER SHEET

There is no doubt that forty-niners who traveled many miles from home to try their hand at gold mining got lonely from time to time. Miners didn't have cell phones to call their families when they needed to share their "I ain't had a bit of luck" or "I struck gold!" stories. They had to write letters instead.

One special kind of letter some miners sent was called a letter sheet. With no digital cameras, miners couldn't send photos, but with letter sheets they could still share the mining experience. Letter sheets included lithograph drawings of mining camp scenes, California cities, the natural wonders of California, and other scenes on one side, and a brief letter could be written on the other side.

"Miners at work with Long Toms" letter sheet.
Bancroft Library, University of California, Berkeley

Materials

Copy paper in white, light blue, or gray
Black pen or pencil
Stamp

☛ Begin by deciding what you would like to draw. If you plan to send your letter to someone in another state or country, you might want to draw a scene from your hometown to illustrate life in your area. Or you can pretend you are a forty-niner and draw a scene from your camp.

Next, decide how you want to lay out your letter sheet. You can fold the paper in half and draw on one half, saving the other "page" for your letter. You can fold the sheet into fourths and draw different scenes on two or three sections and use the other sections for your letter, or you can draw your pictures around the edges of the paper and write within the picture border. Remember to leave one side of your paper blank so you will have a place for the mailing name and address.

Using your pen or pencil, draw your illustrations. Then use the blank spaces to write your letter (If you draw mining pictures, you may want to write your letter about your experiences in the mines). Fold the paper in thirds so that your illustrations and letter are on the inside with the blank page on the outside. Write the receiver's name and address on the blank outside area, and then stamp and mail your letter.

Discrimination in the Mines

Whether a miner panned, used a rocker, or sprayed hydraulic hoses, nothing was easy about gold mining. Nevertheless, persistent prospectors worked on. The next shovelful they dug might uncover the major strike they hoped to find.

But even as hard a life as the miners had, other groups of people suffered much, much more throughout the gold rush years. White prospectors had little tolerance for anyone they considered a foreigner. As potential miners flocked from all over the world in hopes of getting rich, they moved into the Sierra Nevada foothills, forcing out the Native Americans living there. Native people lost their homes as forty-niners staked their claims. Miners destroyed their hunting and fishing grounds. Many of the native people were forced to work for little or no money, and others were murdered simply for getting in the miners' way. An estimated 4,500 Native Americans were violently killed during the early gold rush years.

Although the native people were the most severely persecuted, others groups faced discrimination as well. The foreign miners tax charged foreigners $20 per month for a license to work a mine, a steep payment for most prospectors. After extensive protests, officials lowered the tax to around four dollars, but even that amount proved difficult for most. Latino and Chinese miners were often run out of the mines they worked. At best, white miners pushed them to used-up areas that produced little if any gold.

Life in a Chinese mining camp.
Library of Congress, LC-USZ62-130289

African Americans also endured adversity. Since slavery had not yet been abolished in the United States, slave owners from the South brought their slaves to California to work the mines. At the same time, white prospectors tried to keep blacks from the free states from staking claims, but they couldn't stop them all. Free blacks joined together and mined isolated areas. Like prospectors of all ethnicities, some blacks toiled for days on end with little luck, but others may have struck enough gold to buy family members out of slavery.

Life Outside the Mines

While the majority of people who made their way to California came in search of gold, others chose different methods to make their fortunes. Like

MIFFLIN GIBBS

Mifflin Gibbs sailed from New York to San Francisco in 1850. A carpenter by trade, Gibbs traveled west to see what kind of work might await him. On Gibbs's arrival, a contractor who built houses hired him to work but offered him only $9 a day, rather than the $10 other workers earned. In need of the money, Gibbs accepted, but many of the other employees went on "strike" when Gibbs began working. Gibbs was African American.

Within a short time, Gibbs and a partner opened a successful imported shoe and boot business in San Francisco called Lester & Gibbs. By 1851, Gibbs and a few other black men had started up the *Alto California*, a newspaper that became popular in the state. Through this paper, Gibbs rallied for equal rights for all American citizens.

After a while, Gibbs moved to Canada where he stayed for several years before returning to the United States to earn a law degree. In 1873, Gibbs became the first black municipal judge in the United States. Throughout his life, Gibbs made his own way in the often-unfair world and refused to be held back by oppression and prejudice.

Sam Brannan, many people realized more wealth could be found in supplying miners' needs than in the backbreaking work of looking for gold.

Men made up the majority of people who came to California during the Gold Rush, but some women came, too. Instead of laboring in the mines with the men, many women chose other occupations. These women baked pies and grew vegetables to sell to the hungry, hardworking prospectors. They also took in and washed the filthy miners' clothing for pay.

Some men also looked to areas other than the mines for work. Without ever dipping a pan in the river, a man named Levi Strauss became rich when he started a successful dry goods business selling such items as clothing, underwear, fabric, and, by 1872, a durable new type of pants—blue jeans. Two men by the names of Henry Wells and William Fargo established banks in California and a transport system to protect and ship gold unearthed by prospectors. And in 1852, to help cure the sweet tooth of any miner, Italian immigrant Domingo Ghirardelli began the first chocolate factory in San Francisco.

These enterprising men and women may not have discovered gold, but they did discover that fortunes could be made in California in very different ways.

A New State

In early 1849, California was home to fewer than 20,000 people, but once gold fever struck, that number rose dramatically. By the end of the same year, California's population reached nearly 100,000, and by 1852, it topped 250,000. California's rapid growth occurred with little or no organized government. After the Treaty of Guadalupe Hildalgo was signed in 1848 the California Territory belonged to the United States, but Union officials made no early moves to establish a government there.

Miners had essentially been making their own laws and living by various miners' codes. According to one such code, anyone caught stealing a work animal could be killed by hanging; for lesser thefts, the perpetrator's eyebrows and head could be shaved. The acts of murder and mule killing, both felonies, resulted in a sentence of death. Considering the antiforeigner sentiment during the time, the taking of the law into one's own hands only served to make discrimination worse.

When people realized the need for a civil government, delegates came together in Colton Hall in Monterey to hammer out a state constitution. One of the most important aspects of the constitution noted that California would be a free state—slavery would not be allowed. This issue brought up major questions when the delegates submitted the constitution to the US Congress for approval.

The Union had previously put a compromise in place to guarantee that the number of free states and the number of slave states would always remain equal. If Congress allowed California to enter the Union as a free state, one more free state would exist than slave states. Union officials were concerned that if they upset the balance of states, a civil war might break out.

After a long, heated debate, however, officials reached a decision that included some give and take. The Compromise of 1850 allowed California to enter the Union as a free state, but it also included other provisions that officials hoped would prevent problems between free and non-free states. Some of those provisions included stricter punishment for runaway slaves and allowing New Mexico and Utah to make their own decisions on the issue of slavery. On September 9, 1850, President Millard Fillmore declared statehood for California and allowed it to enter as a free state. Just over one month later, the steamship *Oregon* pulled into San Francisco Harbor. A banner on its side announced the news to Californians: CALIFORNIA IS A STATE.

Mail Call!

Imagine life without telephones, cell phones, text messages, or e-mail. In the mid-1800s, Californians were essentially cut off from the outside world. They knew if they wanted to grow as a state, they needed a better way communicate.

The US Congress helped the state along by passing the Overland California Mail Act in 1857. The federal government awarded a contract to New York businessman John Butterfield that put him in charge of creating a mail route from the eastern United States to California.

Butterfield had his work cut out for him. In order to move mail twice weekly across areas of rugged terrain, Butterfield's crew had to build roads, bridges, and stations. The newly established Overland Mail Company had to purchase stagecoaches, horses, and supplies for the long journey. Butterfield's company spent over a million dollars setting up the mail route, an unheard of amount of money at that time. But the Overland Mail Company took pride in its mission. Butterfield often inspired his employees with these words—"Remember, boys, nothing on God's earth must stop the United States Mail!"

Surprisingly, in only one year's time, Butterfield and his 800 employees established a 2,800-mile route that ran from Saint Louis, Missouri, to San Francisco. But mail delivery still wasn't fast—it took 25 days to deliver. Still, California had established its first major connection to the east.

The Overland Mail Company primarily focused on mail delivery, but some daring souls from the East used the mail coaches as a way of traveling to California. For $200 passengers could board the 24-hour stagecoach as it jostled its way west over the rugged trails, stopping at stations only long enough to change horses. Here's what author Mark Twain had to say in the first volume of his book *Roughing It* about his stagecoach journey with his brother and another passenger:

Overland Mail and Express Company Stage Office.
Library of Congress,
LC-USZ62-50878

> *First we would all lie down in a pile at the forward end of the stage, nearly in a sitting posture, and in a second we would shoot to the other end and stand on our heads. And we would sprawl and kick, too, and ward off ends and corners of mail-bags that*

came lumbering over us and about us; and as the dust rose from the tumult, we would all sneeze in chorus, and the majority of us would grumble, and probably say some hasty thing, like: "Take your elbow out of my ribs! Can't you quit crowding?"

The Pony Express

The Overland Mail Company made a great impact in establishing better communication lines to California, but with threats of Civil War looming, fast communication became even more important.

A year and a half after the Overland Mail Company transported its first delivery to California, a new delivery method was put into place—the Pony Express. Instead of traveling by stagecoach, these adventurous mail carriers rode horseback, the mail tucked safely in saddlebags. When a Pony Express rider climbed into the saddle, he knew he was in for a ride. Relay riding teams covered a 2,000-mile trail, riding a total of about 250 miles in 24 hours. The mail reached its destination in about 9 to 12 days—less than half the time of stage delivery.

The saddlebags of Pony Express's first trip west carried a special message. President James Buchanan sent a note congratulating California's governor on the establishment of the new mail delivery method. Excitement over the Pony Express spread throughout the West. People stood along trails and cheered as the riders sped by.

Celebrations with cannon blasts, fireworks, and official speeches recognized the riders' efforts.

As popular as the Pony Express was, however, the endeavor came to a close at the end of 1861, only about a year and a half after it began. As always, a newer, better, faster communication emerged—the telegraph.

Dot-Dot-Dash

In the mid-1840s, the telegraph began being used in the East as a way for people to communicate over long distances. Telegraphs transmit signals over wire electronically. A telegraph operator in one area would tap out a coded message on the machine in a series of dots and dashes that would be received by an operator in another area; he would then decode the message. It wasn't until 1860, when President James Buchanan signed the Pacific Telegraph Act, that the dream of a transcontinental telegraph line became a reality.

A Pony Express rider gallops past men erecting telegraph lines.
Library of Congress, LC-USZ62-127508

WHISTLE MORSE CODE

Grab a buddy and try sending messages using Morse Code.

Materials

A friend
2 pencils
Paper
2 whistles

☛ For this activity, you and your friend will be in separate areas or rooms.

The first "sender" writes out a word on a piece of paper. Then, using the Morse Code Chart, the sender writes the corresponding dots and dashes under the letters of the word. The sender then uses a whistle to send out his word—dots are quick, short whistles, while dashes are longer whistles.

Go slowly at first and pause in between letters to give the "receiver" time to decode the sounds on paper to spell out the word. After you get the hang of it, swap so the receiver can send messages and the sender can receive.

A	· —	N	— ·
B	— · · ·	O	— — —
C	— · — ·	P	· — — ·
D	— · ·	Q	— — · —
E	·	R	· — ·
F	· · — ·	S	· · ·
G	— — ·	T	—
H	· · · ·	U	· · —
I	· ·	V	· · · —
J	· — — —	W	· — —
K	— · —	X	— · · —
L	· — · ·	Y	— · — —
M	— —	Z	— — · ·

Workers from the East strung wire toward the West, while western builders worked their way eastward. One telegraph linesman, James Gamble, wrote an article that appeared in the *Californian* magazine about his experiences running the lines throughout California:

The telegraph . . . was a source of great curiosity to almost every person along the route, particularly the native population who looked upon the construction of the line with the greatest wonder. Many of them . . . not understanding the use of the poles . . . strung with wire . . . conceived the idea . . . that the Yankees were fencing in the country . . . to keep the devil out.

In October 1861, a cross-country telegraph message sent to Abraham Lincoln from Sacramento stated that the lines to California were complete. The telegraph provided regions from coast to coast with the first high-speed communication system.

War Between the States

In April 1861, as workers stretched telegraph lines across the country, the Civil War erupted. Many of the Southern states wanted to break away from the Union due to disagreements over the issue of slavery. Since California's congressmen had voted in their constitution to prohibit slavery, California joined with the Union cause.

Even by the 1860s, travel to and from California still required major expense and time commitments. Due to these constraints, men from California were not drafted to fight in the battles that took place in the East. The government simply could not afford to bring large numbers of men from the West to join the battles. For the most part during the war, California soldiers spent their time protecting military posts in the West, guarding overland mail deliveries, and monitoring Native American activity.

Some Californians, such as the California 100, the California Column, and the California Battalion did, however, volunteer to engage in battles in the East. And in total, more than 16,000 Californians enlisted to fight for the Union cause.

Transcontinental Railroad

Before, during, and after the war, Congress continued to look for ways to connect California to the rest of the nation. The idea of Manifest Destiny had not been forgotten. Officials still hoped to establish a continental union. Through telegraph usage, communication between the coasts was much faster, but travel time between the East and West was still relatively slow. If citizens and government truly wanted to remedy California's isolation and bring it fully into the union, they would have to come up with a workable plan.

During the 1850s the US railroad system grew rapidly on each side of the country, but up to that point, there had been no common link between the systems. Would a transcontinental railroad be the answer? Could such an immense project ever be agreed upon, financed, and finalized? Would it be possible to find a suitable route over or through the massive and overwhelming Sierra Nevada? One man in particular had faith. He firmly believed these difficulties could be overcome.

Theodore D. Judah

An ambitious, young engineer, Theodore Judah, had no doubt a transcontinental railroad could be achieved. Judah had an impressive reputation in the railroad industry. He had worked on many of the railroad lines in the East and had been brought to California in 1854 to build what would become the first Pacific coast railroad, a railway between Sacramento and Folsom.

The thought of finding the perfect route through the Sierra Nevada for the transcontinental railroad intrigued Judah. In fact, some said he was obsessed with the idea, even crazy. But Judah didn't care. He knew he could play a major role in the establishment of this important means of transportation.

In the late 1850s, a determined Judah developed a plan for building the Pacific railroad. In the plan that he presented to officials in Washington, DC, Judah's enthusiasm for the project was obvious:

The project for construction of a great Railroad through the United States of America, connecting the Atlantic with the Pacific ocean, has been in agitation for over fifteen years. It is the most important project ever conceived. It is an enterprise more important in its bearings and results to the people of the United States, than any other project involving an expenditure of an equal amount of capital. It connects these two great oceans.

Judah's detailed plan caught the interest of many congressmen, but he had more work to do to convince them. The most critical factors involving the railroad were how to pay for the project and the crossing of the 2,000- to 8,000-foot-high passes of the Sierra Nevada. In 1860, Judah set out to find answers to both.

Judah knew that the Sierra Nevada seemed almost insurmountable, but he began surveying the region for various crossing points. Judah searched for an area where only a single ridge would have to be crossed, and he looked for places with long, gradual slopes, rather than steep ascents. After studying numerous routes, Judah found the perfect spot in Donner Pass, near the town of Dutch Flat.

Excited by his discovery, Judah set out to find the financial backing he'd need to set his railway plans in motion. Judah presented his findings to four Sacramento businessmen: Charles Crocker, Mark Hopkins, Collis P. Huntington, and Leland Stanford. Together with Judah, the "Big Four," as they later became known, established the Central Pacific Railroad of California.

By 1862 the federal government readied itself to sign on with the project when it approved the Pacific Railroad Act. The act provided land grants and funds for the project. Judah finally saw some results of all his hard work. His dream of a transcontinental railroad would become a reality.

Sadly for Judah, he and the Big Four had major disagreements. While Judah wanted to construct the railroad wisely and honestly, the Big Four were mostly concerned with making money. They wanted to take construction shortcuts and considered using questionable tactics to increase their personal wealth.

When the Big Four began conducting meetings and making decisions without him, Judah realized he needed to take action. If he could find some partners that would be willing to invest money, Judah could buy the Central Pacific Railroad Company from the Big Four. In 1863, Judah embarked on a trip from California to New York in hopes of finding investors, but as he crossed the Isthmus of Panama on the trip east, he became infected with yellow fever, a disease spread by mosquitoes. Judah died in New York at the age of 37 without seeing the completion of the project in which he'd invested much of his life.

Construction

Building the cross-country railroad would not be an easy undertaking. Workers had to build across a 2,000-mile stretch that included plains, rivers, mountains, and deserts. Since the Civil War still raged, building supervisors would have to find enough men among those not fighting to survey the land, clear and level it, build bridges and tunnels, and lay the track. They had their work cut out for them.

Two companies, the Union Pacific Railroad of the East and the Big Four's Central Pacific Railroad of the West, took on the task. The companies would receive between $16,000 and $48,000 per mile from the federal government for construction, depending on the terrain. Companies would receive less money when building over the flat ground of the plains and more when tackling mountainous regions. Since both companies were interested in making money, they each hoped to lay as many miles of track as possible—the more miles, the more money. With this thought in mind, the race was on. In 1863 the Central Pacific began building east from Sacramento and in 1865 the Union Pacific started laying track westward from Omaha, Nebraska.

Early on, the Union Pacific clipped along laying a mile or two of track each day over the flat Nebraska and Wyoming plains. Workers toiled 10 to 12 hours a day and were paid around two to three dollars for a day's work, plus food and living quarters. Many of the men who worked on the line were immigrants from Ireland who had recently come to America to find work.

After the Civil War ended, many former soldiers also hired on for railroad work. No heavy machinery existed with which to build the railroad—no bulldozers for clearing, no backhoes for loading, no dump trucks for hauling. Every bit of the work had to be completed by hand.

Rail bosses set up assembly-line processes to achieve the most production each day. Engineers

and surveyors worked out front, tapping wooden stakes in the ground to mark the route where tracks were to be laid. Graders came next. With their picks, shovels, and wheeled carts, graders cleared and leveled ground and filled in ditches. In some cases, oxen or horses pulled a piece of equipment called a scraper to help level the earth. Graders did whatever was necessary to ready the land for the tracklayers that followed. Next, horse-drawn wagons carried in the iron rails, ties, connectors, and spikes the tracklayers used. It took about five men to drop the 700-pound rails in place. When everything was ready, the *clank, clank, clank* of a sledgehammer beating in spikes rang through the air securing the rails in place.

As the Union Pacific pushed westward, the Central Pacific labored from the west, heading east. A lack of manpower early on threatened the Central Pacific's progress. California's population

Transcontinental railroad workers hammer in a rail spike.
Library of Congress, LC-DIG-ppmsca-10412

RAILROAD CIPHER

While working on the First Transcontinental Railroad, Central and Union Pacific railroad officials communicated mainly through telegraph transmissions. Since both companies wanted to "beat" the other by laying the most miles of track, they often sent secret, detailed information across the telegraph wires. Each railroad worried that the other company would intercept these messages, so most transmissions were sent in cipher, or code.

The railroads used a substitution cipher, which meant they substituted a word for another word or group of words. For example, they may have used the word "surf" to mean "something is apparently wrong at" and the word "cabbage" to represent the Summit Tunnel. So if someone sent a telegraph message that read "surf cabbage," that cipher would translate to "something is apparently wrong at the Summit Tunnel."

Materials

A friend
2 pencils
2 notebooks

You and your friend will work together to create your own cipher books—just like those used by the railroads. Start by thinking about a couple of messages you might send each other, for example, "Meet me at the oak tree at 4:30."

Break down that message and write it in your cipher book, then come up with substitute words for your message. You could choose a word for the phrase, "meet me at the," another word for "oak tree," and another for "4:30," or you could break up the message in another manner. Whichever you choose, make sure to write down both the broken-down message and the substitution words. This will be your cipher key.

Over time, you can continue to add more messages and more substitution words until you can communicate completely in cipher.

was so small that there simply weren't many workers available. Some men hired on with the railroad, but worked only until they got as far as the gold mining areas. At that point, many quit to discover if they could earn money the "easy" way instead of through backbreaking railroad work.

Central Pacific officials knew they had to do something. With so few workers, they would get little accomplished, and that meant little money would be made. Charles Crocker, one of the Central Pacific's Big Four, made a decision: he would hire Chinese men to do the work.

Thousands of Chinese immigrants had come to California to search for gold. But Chinese life in the mines was difficult—even more difficult than it was for white miners. Not only did they face the physical labor of the mines, they also faced discrimination. Chinese were forced to pay mining and other taxes that white men did not, and they could not vote, become citizens, or attend public school in California. For the most part, white men treated them miserably.

When Crocker made the suggestion that they hire Chinese to work on the railroad, supervisors complained. They thought white workers would not work alongside the Chinese. They also believed Chinese men were too small and weak to perform the difficult labor on the lines. But Crocker held firm. He hired 50 Chinese men as an experiment.

It was soon evident that the Chinese could more than hold their own when performing railroad work. Charles Crocker's brother wrote, "Without them it would be impossible to go on with the work. I can assure you the Chinese are moving the earth and rock rapidly. They prove nearly equal to white men in the amount of labor they perform, and are far more reliable."

By 1868 more than 10,000 Chinese worked for the Central Pacific. Even with the praise they received, the Chinese continued to be discriminated against. While they earned about the same salary as the white workers, they had to set up their own housing and pay for their own food.

The Summit Tunnel

The Chinese proved extremely useful in their work on railroad tunnels. In total, the Central Pacific crews had to build 15 tunnels—all through solid granite—completely by hand.

The construction of the 1,659-foot-long Summit Tunnel seemed almost impossible. Many wondered if it could actually be done. Laborers used picks and hand drills to bore holes into the granite, filled them with a black powder explosive, then lit the fuses to blow out tiny particles and larger chunks of granite. In some places when the black powder was ignited, not a single piece of granite would be blasted out; the granite was simply too hard. During this phase of construction, even with 24-hour workdays, Central Pacific workers measured their progress in only inches a day. To make the work even more difficult, workers fought through dozens of snowstorms.

While working on the tunnels, many Chinese workers participated in an incredibly dangerous procedure. Typically, tunnel workers drilled

Construction of the east portal of the Summit Tunnel in the Sierra Nevada. *Library of Congress, LC-DIG-stereo-1s00547*

SNOW SHEDS

Not only did railroad workers have to deal with the huge amounts of snow that assaulted the Sierra Nevada, trains rolling down the completed tracks did as well.

In his project planning, Theodore Judah had underestimated snowfall amounts in the Sierra. He believed that snowplows on the locomotives would be enough to keep the snow cleared. But that was not the case. During the winters, a full-time crew worked almost continually shoveling snow from the tracks.

Railroad officials knew that if they wanted to keep trains running throughout the winter, they would have to come up with a way to keep the tracks clear of snow. Central Pacific officials decided to build snowsheds over the tracks. These sheds would keep off falling snow and would also divert sliding snow from avalanches.

Material and labor for the more than 35 miles of snowsheds would be outrageously expensive, but the company had no choice; they had to keep the railways open. The final cost of building the sheds topped $2 million, but the snowsheds were effective. They also provided the Central Pacific with an interesting nickname—"railroad in a barn."

from each end of the tunnel with plans to meet in the middle. In the case of the Summit Tunnel, workers not only worked from each end, they also drilled a vertical passage from the top of the mountain so they could work from the center of the tunnel outward. Builders hoped this method would allow them to move at a faster pace.

In order to work through the center passage from the mountaintop, workers lowered baskets holding Chinese laborers into the shaft. The Chinese drilled holes, filled them with black powder, lit the fuse, and were hopefully pulled up before the powder exploded.

Sadly, many Chinese lost their lives from these tunnel-building methods, from accidents, and from avalanches. By the end of 1867 workers completed the Summit Tunnel, amazingly only slightly more than a year after the work had begun.

Race to the Finish

Once Central Pacific laborers made it through the Sierra Nevada, work changed for the better. Flatter land and better conditions allowed workers to move at a much faster pace. They hoped to make up the time lost in the Sierra Nevada. Central Pacific workers knew the Union Pacific was advancing quickly from the east. They had to move fast.

Each railroad company wanted to be the first to arrive in Salt Lake City, Utah. The race continued! Central Pacific workers pushed especially hard. At one point, they set a record by completing 10 miles in a single day.

By spring of 1869, government officials made the decision to have the tracks joined at Promontory, Utah, an area just north of the Great Salt Lake. Although technically the Union Pacific "beat" the Central Pacific by laying the most track, the Central Pacific arrived at Promontory first.

The Golden Spike

On May 10, 1869, the entire United States readied itself for a celebration. After six long, difficult years, the transcontinental railroad tracks would be joined, allowing travelers to journey from one coast to the other in less than a week.

Hundreds of spectators, railroad workers, public officials, and railroad VIPs gathered for the event. When the final two rails were laid, railroad officials grabbed sledgehammers to drive in the final spikes. A telegraph wire had been connected to a spike made from solid California gold, so that when it was struck, telegraph lines would send out the message nationally. Interestingly, when Central Pacific's Leland Stanford aimed for the golden spike, he missed; but that made little difference. The telegraphed message "Done!" was heard around the nation.

Two train engines, the Union Pacific's facing west and the Central Pacific's facing east, pulled together until their front ends touched. All over the United States church bells rang out, cannons blasted, 100-gun salutes erupted, and parades commenced. The dream of a coast-to-coast railway was a reality.

The completion of the transcontinental railroad had lasting effects on California. With fares ranging from about $40 to around $150, the western frontier opened up to more people than ever before. Additionally, the railroad made it faster, easier, and less expensive to transport goods from one part of the country to another.

The new railroad allowed California's economy to grow rapidly. Sadly, for all the good the railroad accomplished, construction also took the lives of many immigrant workers such as the Chinese and had devastating effects on Native Americans who were killed or pushed from their land. Without a doubt, the transcontinental railroad brought major changes, both good and bad, throughout California.

The meeting of the Central and Union Pacific Railroad train engines in Promontory, Utah, upon the completion of the First Transcontinental Railroad. *Library of Congress, LC-USZ62-116354*

SO WHERE IS THAT GOLDEN SPIKE?

Is the golden spike still in the ground in Utah? Nope. Before Stanford hammered in the spike, a hole had already been drilled so it could be easily tapped in and then removed.

Today, the spike inscribed with the words "May God continue the unity of our Country as the Railroad unites the two great Oceans of the world" can be seen at the Cantor Arts Center at Stanford University in Palo Alto, California (http://museum.stanford.edu).

6

Growing Crops, Growing Cities

Even before the completion of the transcontinental railroad, new business ventures had become established in California, particularly in the area of farming. Businessmen realized that the mild climate and fertile land in certain areas of California created perfect growing conditions for many different types of crops. Now the new railroads helped transport the agricultural products, and lower fares enticed more outsiders to explore the state.

California's New Gold

One major agricultural product of the time was considered California's "new gold." This gold didn't come from the mines, however; it came from the fields—wheat. Raw wheat can be ground into flour, a main ingredient in breads, cakes, biscuits, and other foods. It's also used in cereals and pastas.

California's Central Valley, a 450-mile-long by 40- to 60-mile-wide section of land located between the coastal mountains and the Sierra Nevada, made the perfect area for wheat farming. Flat land, rich soil, winter rains, and dry summers all contributed to strong wheat production.

Postcard promoting California's booming citrus industry.
Library of Congress, LC-DIG-ppmsca-19095

For the most part, a few wealthy business-men owned the wheat farms of the Central Valley. Some of these farms consisted of more than 50,000 acres, and all the wheat farms added together totaled more than one million acres by the late 1880s.

California historian Kevin Starr explains what it was like to work on one of these huge farms: workers started out plowing at the end of one field, plowed all day until they reached the other end, and then camped there for the night only to get up the next day and work their way back to where they started. They worked back and forth, back and forth, day in and day out until the entire field was plowed. By 1890, California wheat farms worked this way produced up to 40 million bushels of wheat every year, and that wheat was shipped worldwide.

Farmers in the mid to late 1800s didn't have the sophisticated equipment used for farm work today, but as time went on farmers developed more efficient machinery to help make their work faster and easier. Just like the railroad men, farmers knew if they wanted to make more money, they needed to increase production. They figured if one plow tilling up the land for planting was good, six or eight plows working a row at one time was even better. The gang plow, pulled by eight horses or mules, hitched several plows together so more rows could be plowed in one pass.

New machines, called combines, also went to work. When the wheat was ready for harvest, combines allowed farmers to cut the wheat and separate the seed from the plant all at the same time. The first large combines had to be pulled by a team of 36 horses. Later, steam-powered and gasoline-powered tractors came into being. This new technology allowed farmers to make their land even more productive.

Oranges!

As wheat farming continued its rapid growth, some farmers began looking to establish farms growing other crops. Citrus orchards, growing such fruits as oranges, grapefruit, limes, and lemons began emerging throughout the state.

The first orange trees in California were likely planted at the Spanish missions in the 1760s, but it wasn't until the early 1800s that the citrus

Workers pose for a picture while picking oranges in an orchard near Los Angeles. *Library of Congress, LC-USZ62-26298*

industry began to expand. William Wolfskill became one of the first people to extensively farm citrus fruits when he planted orange and lemon trees on land he obtained near present-day downtown Los Angeles. Wolfskill's operation began as a small orchard of about two acres, but eventually grew to 70 acres.

Early on, Wolfskill sent his oranges northward to San Francisco by ship. Prospectors in the gold mines paid as much as a dollar each for Wolfskill's oranges. Miners knew these fruits were rich in vitamin C, which would help ward off scurvy. For his early contributions to California's citrus production, Wolfskill is sometimes considered the "father of the citrus industry."

Following Wolfskill's lead, other settlers began planting citrus trees. One settler, Eliza Tibbets, had a great impact on California's orange

---

ACTIVITY ➤

USE-THE-WHOLE-ORANGE MUFFINS

California oranges are a great addition to many meals and recipes. For this recipe, you'll use an entire navel orange—the peel and all—along with some juiced oranges, to create some yummy orange muffins.

Adult supervision required

Materials

Muffin tin that will hold 12 muffins
Paper cupcake liners
Knife
3 whole California navel oranges
½ cup
Blender or food processor
1 large egg
½ cup of butter or margarine
2 large bowls
1¾ cup all-purpose flour
¾ cup white sugar
1 teaspoon baking powder
1 teaspoon baking soda
½ to ¾ cup mini chocolate chips, if desired

☞ Preheat oven to 400°F. Line a muffin tin with paper liners.

Halve two oranges and squeeze into a measuring cup until you have ½ cup of juice.

Wash the outside of one large navel orange, but do not peel. With adult assistance, cut the orange into fourths. (If using seeded oranges, remove all seeds.)

Put two of the four orange quarters and the ½ cup of juice into a blender or food processor. (Use caution around processor/blender blades!) Process in the blender or processor until only a thick liquid remains.

Add the other two orange quarters. Process until no chunks remain.

Add the egg and butter to the processor or blender. Mix well.

Pour the orange mixture into a large bowl. In a separate bowl, mix flour, sugar, baking powder, and baking soda.

Add the flour mixture to the orange mixture. Stir until well blended. The batter will be thick. Stir in mini chocolate chips, if desired.

Fill muffin cups about three-fourths of the way full. Bake for 16 to 18 minutes.

Allow to cool, and enjoy!

A *REALLY* GREEN THUMB

William Wolfskill and Eliza Tibbets weren't the only people who had the magic touch when it came to growing things. Luther Burbank wasn't bad himself. When Burbank was only 21 years old and living in Massachusetts, he developed a special kind of potato. The Burbank, or "Idaho" potato as it is more commonly known, was developed in 1871. This potato warded off a plant disease that often affected potatoes. When Burbank sold the rights to his potato for $150, he knew exactly what he would do with the cash: travel to California.

Burbank wanted to leave the wintry weather of the Northeast behind to see if California was truly a plant lover's paradise. When he arrived in Santa Rosa in 1875, Burbank wasn't disappointed. In a letter home he wrote, "I took a long walk to-day and found enough curious plants in a wild spot of about an acre to set a botanist [plant scientist] wild." Burbank also added, "I firmly believe from what I have seen that [California] is the chosen spot of all this earth as far as Nature is concerned."

Burbank spent the majority of his life dedicated to developing the finest plants, flowers, fruits, and vegetables. He often had more than 3,000 different experiments going at one time and worked with millions of plants to make better tasting fruits and vegetables and to make flowers last longer. So the next time you bite into a plum or admire a Shasta daisy, you just might want to thank Mr. Burbank.

Horticulturist Luther Burbank working with flowers in one of his gardens.
Library of Congress, LC-DIG-ggbain-38962

industry. In 1872, not long after moving to California from the East, Tibbets and her husband obtained three orange trees from the US Department of Agriculture. The department agreed to provide the trees because this type of orange had never been grown in California, and officials wanted to see if this variety could thrive there.

Tibbets planted the trees next to her home in Riverside in May 1872 and then carefully watched over her young trees. She wanted to do everything she could to ensure their growth. Even with her close care, Tibbets lost one tree when a cow trampled or chewed it. But the other two survived. Tibbets had to be patient, however. It took five years for her to see the first oranges on her trees—and even then the trees produced only two oranges each. But that was enough.

These navel oranges differed from other oranges of the time. They were large, sweet, easy to peel, and seedless. People declared these new oranges spectacular in every way. Eliza Tibbets' experiment with three tiny plants helped to widely promote California's citrus industry.

Advancing Agriculture

As California agriculture continued to boom with crops such as citrus, grapes, almonds, raisins, beans, and sweet potatoes, orchard and farm owners needed more and more workers to plant, pick, and tend the plants. New ways to transport their goods were also needed.

In considering transportation of their crops, California fruit and vegetable growers often had a problem. They had all this wonderful produce, but how could they get it to buyers across the country before it spoiled?

William Wolfskill and his brother were believed to be the first growers to ship their product east. Loaded on rail cars, the fruit was kept cold by packing it in ice. Due to melting, the ice had to be replaced several times throughout the trip.

By the 1880s a refrigerated rail car had been invented, improving the shipping process even further. At that point, people in places like Saint Louis and Boston enjoyed California's citrus, grapes, apricots, cherries, pears, plums, and other produce, and California became known as a major agricultural area.

Grape picker hard at work in a vineyard in Tulare County, California.
Library of Congress, LC-USZ62-16100

ACTIVITY ➤

GROW A SHASTA DAISY

One of Luther Burbank's best-known flower creations is the Shasta daisy. Try your hand at growing these beauties. Make sure you plant them in the spring, after the danger of frost has passed.

Materials

A sunny location
2 or 3 bricks
12- to 14-inch diameter
   container
Potting soil
Shasta daisy seeds
Fertilizer sticks

☛ Make sure your container has drainage holes in the bottom. Raise the container slightly off the ground by placing it on two or three bricks.

Place the container in an area of full sun, and fill with potting soil. Plant the daisy seeds about a quarter inch deep. Water lightly. Seeds will sprout in two to three weeks.

Whenever the top of the soil begins to feel dry, water lightly. Feed with fertilizer sticks as directed on the package when the seedlings get about three to five inches high. Seeds planted in the spring will produce their first blooms in the summer of the following year. The plants need to be protected during the winter months.

GREAT GRAPES—FAST FACTS

➤ The average American eats eight pounds of grapes every year.

➤ About 98 percent of all grapes produced in the United States are grown in California.

➤ Mission priests probably planted California's very first grapevines.

➤ Remember William Wolfskill, one of California's first citrus growers? Wolfskill was also one of the first Californians to cultivate (farm) grapes.

➤ The San Jaoquin and Coachella Valleys are California's top grape-growing regions.

➤ To make one pound of raisins, four and a half pounds of seedless grapes have to be dried.

➤ Grapes are good for your eyes, your heart, and your brain.

➤ California produces almost two *billion* pounds of table grapes each year.

Growing Cities

As oranges and other fruits and vegetables streamed into the rest of the country, people in other states became more and more aware of California. When California fruit growers shipped their product east, they added colorful labels to the outside of the crates. These labels, with slogans such as "Oranges for Health; California for Wealth," helped promote California agriculture and the state itself.

These labels made people stop and think, I wonder what would happen if I moved to California? Some people saw agricultural opportunities and headed west in hopes of establishing farms. Others flocked westward for the supposed health benefits the state's climate would provide, and others went simply to see what the Wild West had to offer.

Southern California

In the late 1840s, the locations of the gold mines drew people to the area around San Francisco, but Southern California had, for the most part, been left out of this population boom. People believed they could find wealth in the mines, but what could they find in the southern part of the state? How could they even get there? The transcontinental railroad ran to Sacramento in the north, but at that time no railways ran to Southern California. That all changed, however, when the Southern Pacific Railroad steamed into the picture.

It's hard to imagine Los Angeles as a sleepy little town, but it once was. Before the Southern Pacific and another railroad, the Santa Fe, built railways to the south, only about 6,000 people lived in Los Angeles. But these new railroads

PROMOTE IT!

You've read how catchy slogans and brightly colored orange-crate labels tempted people to visit the Golden State. Now see what it takes to create your own advertisement.

Materials

Scratch paper

Pencil

Poster board

Colored markers or poster paints

Decorative items such as construction paper, glitter, puff paint, small items specific to California, magazines, photographs, etc.

Scissors and glue, if needed

Your imagination

☞ Choose a city to promote. It can be your hometown or somewhere you've never even visited. Think about what you would say to someone if you wanted to talk that person into visiting that city. Come up with three to four short, catchy slogans that would convince people to come to the area you've chosen over any other area in the world.

When working on your slogans, consider these questions:

- What are some of the things that make your specific city or area special?
- Why would people want to go there?
- What could they see or do there that they couldn't see or do anywhere else?

If necessary, you can visit your city's website for ideas. Before beginning your poster, choose what you think is the very best slogan—or you may decide to make three separate posters with three different slogans.

Next, come up with a design. What images do you want to use to promote your city? How will you lay out the slogan and the design on your poster? When you decide on your slogan and design, first sketch it out on scratch paper. In creating your design, you may choose to cut out shapes from the construction paper, make a collage with magazine pictures or photographs, or work only with the markers, paints, and decorative items.

Use your supplies to create the perfect advertising poster for your city. It's up to you to bring in new tourists and residents. Go for it!

POPULATION BOOM

This chart shows the amazing growth of the state of California.

YEAR	POPULATION*
1848	14,000
1849	100,000
1852	260,000
1860	379,994
1870	560,247
1880	864,694
1890	1,208,130
1900	1,475,053

These numbers refer to the state's non-Native American population Sadly, during this time, Native Americans were not included in the overall census. However, it is believed that about 150,000 lived in California in 1845. By 1870, that number had dropped to around 30,000.

A NEW METHOD OF TRAVEL

While railroads may have been the most important transportation at the time, a different kind of travel invention was also in the works. As Andrew S. Hallidie made his way around San Francisco, he often watched teams of horses pulling horsecars up the steep streets. Sometimes, particularly when the streets were wet, the horses often struggled and slipped while trying to make their way up the hilly roads.

Hallidie didn't like seeing the horses slip and slide. He didn't like seeing drivers use whips to force the horses up the steep roads, so he set out to do something about it. Hallidie created a system where steam-powered cars, called cable cars, were drawn along a loop of wire rope (cable) running continuously in a slot under the ground.

Early one August morning in 1873, Hallidie and a group of his friends stood at the top of Clay Street. It was time to test the first cable car. The men climbed onto the car and safely rode it to the bottom of the hill. The test was a success! Cable cars became an important part of San Francisco's transportation system until a major earthquake stopped it in its tracks.

The dining car of a train steaming across the United States via the Pacific Railroad.
Library of Congress, LC-USZ62-14133

made travel much easier, and they did something else too; they made travel less expensive.

Each of the various railroads heading west fought for the passengers' business. Each wanted to gain the most riders because more passengers equaled more money. Price wars began. When one railroad offered a $125 fare, another charged $100. If one price dropped to $50, the other would fall to $25. At one point, some railroads charged as little as one dollar!

As you can imagine, competition was a good thing for those interested in heading west. And it was a good thing for the growth of Southern California. By the 1880s, the number of people living in Los Angeles quadrupled to around 24,000, and by 1900, 100,000 people called Los Angeles home.

Trouble in Paradise

As California's population grew, so did its problems. People of all races and nationalities flowed into the state; sadly, many of them didn't get along with each other. Many Americans in California didn't like that people from places such Germany, Ireland, France, or China were hired for jobs that they believed were rightfully theirs. Others didn't like African Americans and Hispanics simply because they had a different skin color. These groups and others faced severe hardship.

View of Los Angeles in the late 1880s.
Library of Congress, LC-USZC4-11554

Life for the Chinese

Many people treated the Chinese unfairly simply because they saw them as different. They wore different kinds of clothes, ate different kinds of food, and practiced different kinds of religion. Many men and boys wore long, braided pigtails called *queues* [KYOOS]. Others disliked the Chinese because they were often willing to work for less money than Americans. If a Chinese man would work for low pay, he would likely be hired over an American who wanted to be paid more. Unemployed white men thought the Chinese were taking jobs away from them.

When Chinese immigrant Andrew Kan came to California in 1880, he witnessed discrimination against the Chinese firsthand:

Chinese treated worse than dog. Oh, it was terrible, terrible, terrible. . . . The hoodlums, roughnecks, and young boys pull your queue, slap your face, throw all kind of vegetables and rotten eggs at you. . . . We were simply terrified; we kept indoors after dark for a fear of being shot in the back. Children spit on us as we passed by and called us rats.

State officials passed laws and ordinances that kept the Chinese from having the same rights as others. One law regulated the size of houses and businesses the Chinese could own. Another forced them to pay higher taxes. The establishment of the "Chinese Quarter" pushed all Chinese to live in a separate area from the other citizens. One California official went so far as to say, "California must be all American or all Chinese. We are resolved that it shall be American, and are prepared to make it so."

Unfortunately, California wasn't the only state that discriminated against the Chinese. In 1882, the US government passed the Chinese Exclusion Act that applied to every state. The act, put in place because officials believed allowing Chinese workers into the country took jobs from Americans, prohibited Chinese workers from entering America for a period of 10 years. Extensions kept portions of the act in force for about 60 years, until it was eventually repealed in 1943.

Despite the hardships the Chinese people faced, they refused to give up on their dreams of a better life. Many started their own businesses, such as grocery stores, restaurants, and laundries in places like Chinatown in San Francisco and led fulfilled lives.

Life in the Fields

With the establishment of huge farms and orchards in California, growers needed good, cheap laborers for planting and harvesting. Many Chinese worked the fields and orchards along with Japanese, Filipinos, and Mexicans.

Day in and day out, these workers faced horrible conditions. Imagine working in the scorching sun for 12 to 16 hours each day and being paid so little that you only had enough for necessities. And instead of spending nights in a comfortable home, you'd sleep in a tent near the fields so you would be ready to head back to work at sunup.

Latinos often worked on farms simply because no one would hire them to do anything else. They lived apart from white Americans and celebrated their culture in Spanish-speaking towns called *barrios*.

Native American laborers also found work in agriculture. Like the others, they received little money for their work and had to fight even for a place to live. Many were forced to live on reservations, land that the US government set aside for them.

Chinese children in San Francisco. Note the child's long pigtail, or queue. *Library of Congress, LC-USZ62-56607*

Few African Americans, only about 7,800, called California home in the late 1800s. While some labored on farms, many worked in towns and cities. African Americans also experienced discrimination and could usually only obtain low-paying jobs.

Even though life was extremely difficult for many new Californians, most of them did not pack up and head back home. Even with the hardships they faced, they saw California as a land of opportunity. They refused to give up on their dreams too easily. Most believed if they stuck with it, they would find a better life in the Golden State.

THE PIGTAIL ORDINANCE

As another way to discriminate against Chinese, in 1873 officials of San Francisco put a regulation in place that stated that Chinese men and boys could not wear their traditional long braid, or queue. Since the queue is an important part of Chinese culture, the Chinese felt great shame to have the braid cut off. Additionally, the ordinance required any Chinese prisoner in a San Francisco jail to have not only his braid removed, but to have his hair cut to one inch in length. Fortunately, the ordinance was dropped when a court eventually ruled the practice unfair since it applied only to the Chinese.

7

A New Century

The 1800s brought major changes throughout California. The Spanish missions closed, Mexican Californio ranchos were established, gold was discovered, and the territory became an American state. The population then boomed with the coming of the transcontinental railroad and new agricultural ventures. How could the state ever top that? Would the 20th century bring extensive changes? Would those changes be good? Bad? Or both?

San Francisco Devastation

By 1906 San Francisco had become a bustling city—the largest city on the Pacific coast and the ninth largest city in the United States. Tall office buildings, fine restaurants, stately churches, fancy hotels, theatres and opera houses, department stores, small factories, and businesses of all kinds lined the streets. The US Mint, the largest mint in the world, holding more than $200 million dollars in gold, was also located there. San Francisco had five daily newspapers and more than 40 banks. This once quiet town had blossomed into a full-fledged city.

All that changed, however, in April 1906. It was a day of tragedy that Californians would never forget. Businessman Peter Bacigalupi had this to say about the natural disaster that took place shortly after five o'clock in the morning on April 18, 1906:

San Francisco houses tilt on their frames after the 1906 earthquake.
Library of Congress, LC-DIG-ppmsca-09834

On the morning of the 18th of April I was awakened from a sound slumber by a terrific trembling, which acted in the same manner as would a bucking broncho [sic]. I sat up in bed with a start. My bed was going up and down in all four directions at once, while all about me I heard screams, wails, and crashing of breaking china-ware and nick-nacks. I was very quietly watching the clock on the mantel, which was doing a fancy stunt, while the ornaments in the parlor could be heard crashing to the floor. A great portion of plaster right over the head of my bed fell all around me, and caused a cloud of dust, which was very hard to breathe through. I did not get up until the quake was over, then dressed in a hurry, with the thought in mind that there must have been a great deal of damage done down town.

San Francisco burning as a result of the 1906 quake.
Library of Congress, LC-USZ62-44926

What woke Bacigalupi and about 400,000 other San Francisco residents up was an earthquake later estimated to be an 8.3 magnitude. And Bacigalupi was right—a great deal of damage *had* been done by the quake that had been felt from Southern Oregon to Los Angeles.

As survivors crawled from their homes into the darkened streets, they were shocked by what they saw. Chimneys had crumbled onto the ground next to homes, water pipes and gas lines had ruptured, extensive cracks stretched along cobblestone roads, brick buildings lay crumbled in the streets, and what was left of City Hall peeked from the rubble. As daylight dawned, San Franciscans barely recognized Market Street—a place where many had ridden cable cars, worked, or dined. And the rest of the city was no better. Much of San Francisco had been demolished by the quake.

San Franciscans who had lost their homes wandered the streets. A reporter for the *Call-Chronicle Examiner*, a city newspaper, wrote:

Thousands of the homeless were making their way with their blankets and scant provisions to Golden Gate Park and the beach to find shelter. Those in homes on the hills just north of the Hayes Valley wrecked section piled their belongings in the streets. . . . Everybody in San Francisco is prepared to leave the city, for the belief is firm that San Francisco will be totally destroyed.

PACK AN EARTHQUAKE PREPAREDNESS KIT

Earthquakes are a fact of life for California residents. Fortunately, today's structures are built to withstand quakes much better than buildings of long ago. Even so, it's important to be prepared. These supplies may seem like a lot to gather, but they can save lives.

Materials

Large plastic boxes with lids, on rollers if possible (the number of boxes you'll need depends on the size of your family)

PROVISIONS

Water, one gallon per person per day—at least a 3-day supply (store-bought bottled water is recommended for safety). Add additional water for pets, too.

Canned meat, soups, and vegetables

Manual can opener

Canned juices

Snacks: crackers, peanut butter, granola bars, cookies

FIRST AID KIT

Adhesive bandages

Gauze pads in various sizes

Adhesive cloth tape

Antibiotic/antiseptic cream or ointment

Premoistened towelettes

Latex gloves

Tweezers

Thermometer

Essential medications

Nonprescription pain relievers

SUPPLIES

Flashlight with extra batteries

Portable radio with extra batteries

Candles

Matches in a waterproof container

Fire extinguisher

Adjustable wrench to turn off gas and water

Whistle to signal for help

Plastic plates, bowls, cups, and utensils

Garbage bags

PET SUPPLIES

Extra water for pets

Pet food

Leash

☛ Separate the items by category and pack them in the large plastic boxes. Store the boxes in a predetermined area so that all family members will know where they are located in case of an emergency. It is preferable to store the boxes in a secure outdoor location, such as a garage or garden shed, since it may not be safe to return indoors due to damage and/or aftershocks.

Just when people thought things couldn't get worse, they did. Ruptured gas lines, overturned stoves, and fallen electrical wires caused a problem that would prove worse than the quake itself—fires.

Flames shot high into the air, and the sky filled with clouds of thick, black smoke. As fires erupted across the city there was little anyone could do. Many of the city's fire departments had been damaged by the quake, and even if firefighters could get to the burning areas, they had little or no water to put out the fires. Most of the water mains had broken during the quake, spilling the precious water onto the ground.

For three days the fires raged. They rapidly spread to South of Market, up Van Ness Avenue, and across Gough Street, before racing up Nob Hill.

Without water, how could the fires be stopped? How could what was left of San Francisco be saved? Officials decided to take drastic steps. They chose to use dynamite to create firebreaks. Officials believed the spread of the fire could be stopped if areas of brick and other rubble from buildings were piled up to form a sort of barrier.

Horse-drawn wagons loaded with dynamite arrived at the business district, and blasting began. Unfortunately, blasting the buildings did little to stop the fire, and in some cases may have even made it worse. Thankfully, after three days, the blazes began to burn themselves out.

When the final damage reports came in, the quake and resulting fire had destroyed 28,000 buildings, not only in San Francisco but also in surrounding areas such as Santa Rosa and San Jose. About one-half of San Francisco's residents no longer had homes. Even more tragic than the loss of property was the loss of life. At the time the event took place, officials estimated that about 300 to 400 people died. Today, many historians believe that the death toll rose to more than 3,000, with some estimates as high as 6,000. These historians believe that the toll originally overlooked the deaths of many Chinese, Irish, and Japanese workers, and that it did not include deaths that occurred in the following year that were caused by earthquake injuries. Additionally, many now believe that at the time of the quake, city officials did not want to reveal the actual death toll because they thought it would cause panic among residents and would damage San Francisco's reputation.

(left) Proclamation poster by San Francisco Mayor E. E. Schmitz stating the penalty for those found looting homes or businesses after the 1906 quake.
Library of Congress, Printed Ephemera Collection, Portfolio 2, Folder 25

(right) Destruction of San Francisco as seen from Telegraph Hill.
Library of Congress, LC-USZ62-47591

As one eyewitness traveled through the city, he wrote:

> *One was accustomed to the full-toned voice of a big city, intensified by traffic over the cobbles of Market Street, the strident cries of newsboys, the clanging of car bells. All of these are silent: the noises are those of a village—the wagons, carts, and men on horseback, screened against a ghastly background.*

Many believed the once beautiful city would never again exist. But they were wrong. Aid such as tents, food, and supplies came in from different areas of the country, and President Theodore Roosevelt sent army troops and money to help the city get back on its feet. San Franciscans wouldn't rest until their city and their lives were rebuilt.

John Muir

Before San Francisco's crisis, a man named John Muir had sailed into the city. As soon as he climbed off the ship, he stopped to ask directions. When asked where he wanted to go, Muir replied, "Anywhere that is wild."

Muir, a naturalist, had always had a keen interest in nature and the outdoors, and when he arrived in California in 1868 he knew he'd found his paradise. After only a short time in California, Muir discovered the glories of Yosemite, a vast wilderness area in the east central part of the state. He studied its sequoia, spruce, and cedar trees; granite cliffs and ridgelines; Sierra Nevada streams, waterfalls, and wildlife. Even today, people flock to the area to hike, fish, rock climb, bird-watch, and to view the meadows and unusual rock formations found in Yosemite Valley, the giant sequoias in Mariposa Grove, and the astounding views from Glacier Point.

John Muir knew that as cities continued to expand, much of the natural environment would be lost. He wanted to do what he could to preserve California's wilderness. One of his first missions was the founding of the Sierra Club, an organization that works still today to protect our planet's environment and natural spaces. Muir and his group wanted everyone to know about California's beauty, and they wanted to make sure it would be protected.

In 1903 Muir had a very special guest join him on a camping trip to Yosemite—the president of the United States. Throughout his life, Theodore Roosevelt had been an avid outdoorsman and, like Muir, believed in the importance of protecting America's natural areas.

When the president arrived in California, he and Muir set off for Yosemite on horseback. As they traveled the snow-covered ground, Muir and Roosevelt took in the beauty of the area and talked of the importance of keeping Yosemite unspoiled. The men spent the night at Glacier Point, and then rode to Nevada Falls the next day. Roosevelt, a bird-watcher, pointed out interesting birds he saw along the trail, and Muir told the president about plants and trees unique to the area.

The four days the president spent in Yosemite had a major impact on him. Only one day after his trip, Roosevelt said, "We are not building this country of ours for a day. It is to last through the ages." And in a speech he gave later, Roosevelt said:

Naturalist John Muir with President Theodore Roosevelt on Glacier Point in Yosemite Valley (1903). *Library of Congress, LC-USZC4-4698*

Lying out at night under those giant sequoias was like lying in a temple built by no hand of man, a temple grander than any human architect could by any possibility build, and I hope for preservation of the groves of giant trees simply because it would be a shame to our civilization to let them disappear. They are monuments in themselves.

A short time later, thanks to the work of Muir and President Roosevelt, the federal government took control of Yosemite and Mariposa Grove and designated them national parks. National parks are areas set aside by the government for people to enjoy and where hunting, mining, logging, and most development are banned or restricted. The designation of America's national parks ensures that regions of majestic beauty remain unspoiled for generations to come.

Even after Muir helped get his beloved Yosemite protected, he still had more to do to safeguard the park. In the early 1900s, with San Francisco's rapid growth, officials needed to find a significant water source for the city. And after the 1906 earthquake and fire, the need for water became even more important. Residents became worried. What if something like this happened again? What could they do to be prepared? Officials needed to find a nearby water source where water could be stored in case of another disaster.

In searching the area near San Francisco, they had an idea. If they built a dam on the Tuolumne

BECOME A BACKYARD SCIENTIST

John Muir spent most of his life enjoying, studying, and analyzing nature. He recognized the fragile beauty of the natural world and understood the importance of conserving the exquisite life that surrounds us. How can you follow in Muir's footsteps?

Today, various organizations need volunteers to help them collect data for studying facets of nature—insects, plants, animals, etc. And the cool thing about it is you don't have to be an actual scientist in order to participate. These organizations need people just like you and me so that they can obtain a wide sample of results with which to conduct their studies.

Take a page from Muir's book and see how you can participate.

Materials

Computer access
Various supplies, depending on the particular project

☛ Start out by entering the words, "Citizen Science" and the name of your state into a search engine such as Yahoo!, Google, or Bing. The search results should bring up a number of citizen science projects with directions on how to go about participating.

You may find projects that deal with such activities as tracking weather patterns, studying tide pools, planting sunflowers, or counting honeybees, birds, or sea otters. The site will include specific instructions about how data is to be collected and reported. Choose the one you find most interesting, and get to work!

FOR NATIONAL PROGRAMS, SEE:

Community Collaborative Rain, Hail, and Snow Network
www.cocorahs.org

The Great Backyard Bird Count
www.birdsource.org

National Wildlife Federation
www.nwf.org/Wildlife/Wildlife-Conservation/Citizen-Science/Citizen-Science-Programs.aspx

FOR CALIFORNIA-SPECIFIC PROJECTS, TAKE A LOOK AT THE FOLLOWING:

California Academy of Sciences
www.calacademy.org/science/citizen_science/

Californian Avian Data Center
http://data.prbo.org/cadc2/index.php?page=citizen-science-activities-throughout-california

The Anza Borrego Foundation
http://theabf.org/research/citizen_science

You may also want to contact local museums to find out about any ongoing projects.

River in Yosemite, the Hetch Hetchy Valley would become a great flooded reservoir. With all this available water, the growing city would have all it needed for everyday life, and it would also be available in case of another disaster. Sounds like the perfect plan, right?

Not to John Muir. Muir and the Sierra Club worried about what damming the river would do to the beautiful Hetch Hetchy Valley. If water flooded the valley, the animals, birds, and insects that lived there would lose their homes. Trees, flowers, and grasses would be destroyed.

Muir and the Sierra Club weren't going to give up without a fight. They talked to people and urged them to write letters to their congressmen. They wrote essays, made speeches, and gave interviews to newspapers to make readers aware of what would happen to the valley. Muir and the Sierra Club fought against the damming of the river for several years, but residents of San Francisco voted in favor of the project. In 1913, the federal government approved its construction.

Sadly, Muir became ill and died a short time later, but today the Sierra Club still hasn't given up its fight. They may have lost the first battle, but they continue to work to regain Hetch Hetchy Valley. The Hetch Hetchy Valley Restoration Task Force still works to have the dam removed and to return the valley to its original beauty. Muir's dedication lives on.

Like San Francisco, other growing California cities had water concerns of their own. In the early 1900s, Los Angeles was literally running out of water, which was a major problem. As with other cities in California, Los Angeles had experienced a huge amount of growth. People had flocked to the area to enjoy all the benefits it had to offer including agricultural work and employment in the canning, packing, and shipping industries. The population of Los Angeles had grown to around 200,000 by the early 1900s. There was no way the closest water source, the Los Angeles River, could keep up with the demand.

Something had to be done, and city officials came up with a plan. They looked to the eastern part of the state, to the Owens River. But this river was over 200 miles away and across mountains and deserts. They would need to build a giant pipe called an aqueduct to carry water from Owens River to Los Angeles. Building the aqueduct wouldn't be easy, and farmers in Owens Valley fought against the project because it would use up much of the water they needed for their crops. But the aqueduct went through. In 1913 water gushed from the pipe. Los Angeles had water.

Lights, Camera, Action!

After the turn of the century, Californians, like other Americans, discovered an exciting new pastime—the movies! These movies weren't anything close to the blockbusters we watch on the big screen today. They weren't in color, had no sound, and cost only five cents admission. A live piano player set the mood for the movie by playing spooky music during scary parts, lively music for action scenes, and slow music during sad parts. These first movies usually lasted fewer than 15 minutes, and the "theatres" were in no way fancy, but moviegoers were hooked. These first motion picture establishments were called nickelodeons, and they were only the beginning.

As more and more people spent their spare time (and money!) at nickelodeons, studios worked to find newer and better ways to produce movies. After a time, the five-cent movies began to be replaced by longer, more sophisticated movies called feature films—and this is where California really shone. Moviemakers soon discovered that California's mild climate and gorgeous scenery made it the perfect place to shoot their movies, so several of them packed their cameras and headed west.

Actors on a Hollywood film set in 1923.
Library of Congress, LC-USZ62-131093

ACTIVITY

PRODUCE YOUR OWN MOVIE

Hollywood is known for its movies. Why not try making one of your own?

Materials

Pencil and paper
Actors
Props
Costumes
Video camera
Computer (optional)
Popcorn

☛ Think about the historical events you've read about so far—would it be interesting to be a gold miner, a worker on the transcontinental railroad, an explorer, an emigrant, or some other figure in California history? Choose a topic that interests you and brainstorm how you might turn that idea into a movie.

Begin working on a script. It's often best to begin with a character that has a problem. The character's attempt at solving this problem will be your film's plot. Make sure your script has a distinct beginning, middle, and end. The story also needs lots of action to keep it interesting. Start short at first; you can always add more scenes if necessary.

When your script is complete, make up a storyboard that shows the movie's layout. Fold a sheet of paper in half, then in half again, then in half one more time. The fold creases will divide your paper into eight squares. In each square, sketch an image of what will take place in that particular scene. Also, write brief notes about what's happening in each scene. Use more paper as needed. The storyboard will help you visualize your story as a whole.

Gather necessary props, actors, and costumes. Find a great location, and begin shooting your film. When your movie is finished, you can either connect it to a television to show it, or upload the movie to a computer. If uploading to a computer, use movie software to add the finishing touches. Grab a bowl of popcorn and enjoy!

HOLLYWOOD HANDPRINTS

Grauman's Chinese Theatre in Hollywood is a famous theatre, but it's also known for the space that exists out front. Since the 1920s, movie stars have imprinted their handprints and footprints in cement.

Make your own handprint stepping stone, just like the stars!

Adult supervision required

Materials

Protective eye goggles
Dust mask
1½ to 2 cups water
Bucket
10-pound bag cement mix
Wooden paint stirrer or small trowel
9-inch by 13-inch aluminum foil baking pan
Pencil or screwdriver
Small items such as seashells, polished stones, fake jewels, buttons, etc., if desired

☞ Before mixing the concrete, put on safety goggles and dust mask. Pour 1½ cups of water into the bucket. With the paint stirrer or trowel, gradually stir in the concrete mix (you may not need the entire bag). Add more water if needed to make a heavy mud consistency.

When thoroughly mixed, pour moistened concrete into a foil pan. Smooth the concrete surface with the trowel or paint stirrer. Wait about five minutes and then press your hand into the concrete. Press down and wiggle your hand back and forth slightly to get a good impression. If your handprint looks good, leave it, but if you'd like another try, smooth out the surface

with the trowel and do it again. Repeat this step with your other hand. When satisfied, immediately wash your hands with soap and water. Rinse well.

If you'd like, you can write your name, the date, or other information using a pencil or screwdriver. You can also press some decorative items into the concrete, if desired. Thoroughly wash the bucket, trowel, screwdriver, and other equipment. Allow the concrete to dry completely—it may take two to three days or more. When completely dry, pop your creation out of the foil pan. Your creation will make a great outdoor stepping-stone.

Hundreds of hand and feet prints line the forecourt of Grauman's Chinese Theatre including not only the handprints of famous cowboy Roy Rogers, but his horse Trigger's hoofprints as well.
Library of Congress, LC-DIG-highsm-04042

LIONS AND TIGERS AND BEARS

While some were headed to the movie theatre, a doctor named Harry Wegeforth was busy establishing a fun, new way for Californians to spend their time.

Back in 1916 California was celebrating the opening of the Panama Canal with

A panda rests on a tree limb at the San Diego Zoo.
Library of Congress, LC-DIG-highsm-05002

a big celebration. The Panama-California International Exposition, held in San Diego's Balboa Park, brought in lots of visitors and lots of exotic animals for those visitors to see. One day during the exposition, Wegeforth drove down Sixth Avenue and heard a most interesting sound—a lion's roar. This got the animal-loving doctor thinking about establishing a zoo in San Diego.

In no time at all, Wegeforth had a plan. He gained approval from the city, found a location, gathered donations, and then began the fun part: locating the animals. A pet bear named Caesar was one of the San Diego Zoo's first animals. As the story goes,

no one was exactly sure how to get the bear to the zoo. When it came time to move her (Caesar was a female bear), they slipped a collar around her neck, placed her in the front seat of a car, and drove her to her new home. Later, when some elephants came in from India, Wegeforth and others simply rode them to the zoo. What a sight that must have been!

Today the 100-acre San Diego Zoo is home to more than 4,000 animals. Over three million people visit the zoo each year. A special plaque at the top of Wegeforth Bowl stadium recognizes Dr. Wegeforth's efforts. And it all started with a single roar!

Hollywood became *the* place to make movies. Studios such as Disney, Paramount, and Warner Brothers sprang up in California, as did fancy theatres such as the Million Dollar Theatre on South Broadway in Los Angeles and the famous Grauman's Chinese Theatre on Hollywood Boulevard.

By the mid-1920s, "talkies" were born—movies had sound! This new improvement made even more people want to go to the movies. Hollywood film studios produced Westerns, animated cartoons, musicals, and "pie-in-your-face" comedies. Stars like Clark Gable and Greta Garbo graced the screen, and movies such as Mickey Mouse's *Steamboat Willie* thrilled audiences. Visitors came to Hollywood from all over the world in hopes of catching a glimpse of their favorite movie stars. Hollywood's young movie industry was just beginning, and it would continue to grow to become a grand part of California's history and economy.

THE HOLLYWOOD SIGN

One of the most photographed landmarks in the world is the Hollywood Sign perched atop Mount Lee. When it was first erected in 1923, the sign read HOLLYWOODLAND. The sign was originally constructed as a giant advertisement to sell land and houses in a subdivision. It wasn't until 1949 when repairs were made that the "land" part of the sign was removed.

And just how giant is it? Today, each letter is 50 feet high—that's the height of five basketball goals stacked end to end.

Black Gold

As the movie industry boomed, another California industry also gained steam. You could say it was the third "gold" found in California after genuine gold and wheat. It was oil.

People had been using oil found in California since early Native Americans used the asphaltum they discovered to waterproof their baskets and canoes. But it wasn't until the early 1900s that the industry really took off. Major oil (or petroleum) deposits found in Bakersfield, Elk Hills, Long Beach, and other areas thrust California into the oil spotlight.

Oil is important because it is used to make gasoline and diesel fuels that run automobiles, tractors, and other equipment and machines. Today petroleum can be found in plastics, crayons, deodorants, DVDs, and even bubble gum! By 1920, California produced over 100 million barrels of oil.

The early 1900s was the perfect time for the California oil boom to occur. California roads were becoming filled with more and more automobiles. And, of course, those autos needed gasoline to keep them running.

In those days, no gas stations existed. People wanting to fill up had to drop by a local hardware or drugstore where they paid about 60 cents a gallon for fuel, about $13 a gallon in today's dollars. Since gas was sometimes difficult to find, many drivers carried a couple of filled gas cans with them when they traveled, which would be considered very dangerous today. More cars led to more and better roadways, and better roadways led to more tourists. California's great growth continued.

A gusher spews oil in California in 1910.
Library of Congress, LC-USZ62-124337

THE OIL QUEEN

When you think of oil fields, you might think of gushers bursting into the air; grimy, oil-covered men; and slick businessmen making deals—but this wasn't always the case. One famous oil businessman was in fact a business*woman*.

Emma Summers wasn't your typical oil tycoon. She was a woman, and she was also a music teacher. Who would think she could make a fortune in oil? But she did. Emma became caught up in the oil excitement when she lived near the Los Angeles City Oil Field. Emma invested $700 in a well near today's Dodger Stadium, but that venture failed and she lost her money.

But Emma wasn't ready to give up. She believed in herself. She once said, "I would not take even the greatest lawyer's opinion unless it squared with my own convictions." Emma borrowed money and invested in other wells. By the early 1900s Emma owned and operated 14 wells of her own that produced about 50,000 barrels each month. The music teacher and unlikely oilwoman became known as "California's Oil Queen."

ANGEL ISLAND

Even with the widespread growth, Californians, for the most part, were still intolerant of people of different races. Distrust and dislike of the Chinese in particular continued. With immigrant exclusion acts still in place, the US government allowed only a certain number of Chinese laborers to enter the United States each year.

In 1910 a station sometimes called the "Guardian of the Western Gate" was constructed on Angel Island, the largest island in San Francisco Bay. As ships came in from all over the world, their immigrant passengers had to be cleared before they could enter the country. In many cases, immigration officials refused entry to the Chinese. Many Chinese immigrants were held in prison-like conditions for days, months, or even years because they could not officially prove they had the right to be there.

While at the station the Chinese looked for ways to spend the long hours. Some expressed their sadness and frustrations by carving poems onto the walls of their living quarters at the station. One of the poems begins, "Imprisoned in the wooden building day after day, / My freedom withheld; how can I bear to talk about it?"

The Angel Island Immigration Station closed in 1940 after one of its main buildings burned. It was not until the enactment of the Immigration Act of 1965 that Chinese immigrants were freely allowed to enter the United States.

8

Difficult Times

At the turn of the century, California thrived. San Francisco was rapidly being rebuilt. The movie industry, oil fields, and agriculture continued their growth. People flocked to the state, both to visit and to live. Life in the Golden State was pretty nice.

Sadly, that happiness wouldn't last. Two events on the horizon would bring many changes to the lives of all Americans. How would Californians cope with the devastating events of the Great Depression and World War II? Would they be able to keep the California dream alive through such tragedy?

The Great Depression

October 29, 1929, a day that would be remembered as "Black Tuesday," changed the lives of all Americans. On that day the US economy took a major tumble. The stock market crashed, setting off a crisis that would last for more than 10 years. Businesses, banks, manufacturing plants, and farms closed down. Workers all over the United States lost their jobs. With no money coming in, many lost their homes as well. Most did not have money to buy food, clothing, or even necessary medicine.

Family leaving Oklahoma in search of a better life in California.
Library of Congress, LC-USF33-012312-M1

For Californians who had been living with prosperity and success, the Depression came as an unbelievable shock. Many stood in long lines in front of soup kitchens just to get a little bread and other food for their families to eat. Unable to make the payments on their homes, families were forced to live in makeshift shelters in parks and other areas. People pitched tents or built rickety shacks out of whatever scrap material they could find.

In Oakland, some actually lived inside six-foot-long concrete pipes that were being stored on property near 19th Avenue. A reporter for the *Oakland Post Inquirer* wrote that in order to qualify to live in this "Pipe City," a person had to be "jobless, homeless, hungry, and preferably shoeless, coatless, and hatless. If one also is discouraged, lonely, filled with a terrible feeling of hopelessness and helplessness, one's qualifications are that much stronger."

"The Black Blizzard"

Just when things looked like they couldn't get any worse for Americans, they did. Events taking place more than 1,000 miles from the Golden State would greatly affect California. Hot, dry weather had plagued states such as Kansas, Oklahoma, Texas, Arkansas, and other regions of the Midwest and Southwest for several years.

Farmers didn't have enough water to keep their crops alive. When the crops died, nothing remained but bare ground. Giant windstorms blew across the barrenness, sending huge clouds of dust through the air. The thick dust covered everything in sight.

Winton Slagle Sipe remembered living through one of the many dust storms that hit Kansas:

The clouds were very dark and appeared to be solid and rolling on the ground as they approached from the southwest. . . . [At one point they] completely blocked out the sun, and it was very dark and eerie. As we started to the house a few large drops of muddy rain fell, and then the dust and wind reached us. Before we got to the house, the air was so full of dust we could not open our eyes and could hardly breathe. The storm lasted all night, and when we got up the next morning there was about an inch of fine, red dust on everything in the house. . . . The dust drifted like snow. It was drifted about eighteen inches deep on the northeast side of all the buildings, and every fence post, tree, and weed had a long, pointed drift on its northeast side.

Dust storms rolled in one after another. Farmers who lived in the states that became known as the Dust Bowl had no income. The drought had withered their crops and parched the land. Farmers didn't know what to do—they had no work, yet they still had families to feed. They had no way to make payments on their homes and land. Many, perhaps as many as 200,000, made a decision. They decided to head west to California.

In Search of a Better Life

Just like thousands of people before them, farmers who had lost their farms and homes in the Dust Bowl looked to California to find better lives. They had heard about California's mild climate, and many believed this was the place to make a fresh start. All they needed was a piece of ground, some California sun, and a little luck, and they'd be on their way. Or even if they weren't able to have their own farm right away, with all of California's established farms, plenty of work should be available. At least they thought it would be that easy. Sadly, it was not.

The Dust Bowl families, "Okies" as they became known, heaped their belongings onto the backs of trucks or atop cars—mattresses, furniture, cook stoves, washtubs, food such as bacon, potatoes, and bags of flour or meal filled every last nook and cranny. With everything loaded and tied down, each family member scouted out a cramped hole or corner where they could ride, and the adventure began.

They knew the trip wouldn't be easy, but most were optimistic about beginning a new life in California. Loaded-down trucks and Model Ts rolled down Route 66, a major roadway that led to California. The travelers struggled with overheated engines, flat tires, and trying to save what little money they had, but after about a two-week journey many Okies saw California for the very first time.

A Not-So-Warm Welcome

Many Dust Bowl emigrants had seen fliers, called handbills, that advertised job opportunities in agricultural regions of California. Big farms in places such as the San Joaquin Valley, Imperial Valley, and Salinas Valley needed workers to pick crops such as peas, cotton, strawberries, beans, and oranges. Some emigrants found work on these farms, but were paid little—often less than $1.50 per day, less than $20 in today's dollars. Others didn't find any work at all.

By the late 1930s, so many emigrants had flooded into the state that farms had more workers than they needed. Since Californians had

Photographer Dorothea Lange took this photo of an Arkansas squatter living in a makeshift shelter near Bakersfield in 1935.
Franklin D. Roosevelt Library Digital Archives

CREATE A PHOTO ESSAY

Photographers Dorothea Lange and Ansel Adams spent a great deal of time photographing people and places in California. Lange captured the troubles faced by the Dust Bowl emigrants, and Adams documented life in the Japanese internment camp at Manzanar. Both Lange and Adams wanted people to be aware of what was happening during these events. Their photographs tell a wordless story of what life was like for the emigrants and the internees.

Try your hand at making your own photo essay.

Materials

Paper
Pencil
Digital camera
Computer with a presentation program
    such as PowerPoint or Keynote (optional)
Computer printer (optional)

For computer method:
Binder with clear pocket on front
Page protectors

For traditional method:
Scrapbook with a plain front
Glue or double-sided tape
Cardstock or stick-on letters

☛ Using the pencil and paper, brainstorm a list of things that are important to you. Choose the one you think you could best illustrate through photographs. Remember, with a photo essay you want to be able to tell a story with the images you include.

As you shoot your photos, use various methods such as extreme close-ups, wide-angle shots, or even photos taken at various angles. Mix it up to keep your photos interesting, and don't try to include too much in each photo.

COMPUTER METHOD

Upload your images to a computer. Decide in which order the photos best tell your story. Using the presentation software, design your photo essay. Short, two- or three-sentence captions are OK, but remember to let the pictures tell the story.

Print your essay, place sheets in clear sheet protectors, and snap into your binder. Design a cover with an interesting title, print it, and place it in the binder's front pocket. Share!

TRADITIONAL METHOD

Have your photos processed and printed at a local business. Lay out the photos and decide in which order they best tell your story. Using the glue or tape, stick your photos to the scrapbook pages. You may wish to write short, two- or three-sentence captions beneath your photos, but remember to let the pictures tell the story. Print an interesting title on cardstock and glue or tape it to the front cover, or create your title with stick-on letters. Share!

been affected by the Depression just like everyone else, many decided they didn't want these "Okies" coming in and taking their jobs.

To stop the flow of emigrants, California officials began turning new arrivals back when they reached the state's border. A group of Los Angeles police officers called the "bum brigade" refused to let emigrants enter their city. In order to get the emigrants to leave, some California residents called them hurtful names, beat them up, and burned down the temporary shacks in which they lived. They posted signs that read, "NO JOBS in California. If YOU are looking for work—KEEP OUT."

Dust Bowl emigrants had come to California looking for a better life. Many stayed and made the best of what they had, but others left as bad or worse off than they had been before.

During the Great Depression, life was hard everywhere. With few jobs, scarce food, and little hope, Americans began to wonder if life would ever get better. But in 1933, things began to change when Americans elected Franklin Delano Roosevelt as their 32nd president.

Bright Spots

President Roosevelt had a plan that he called the New Deal that he believed would bring the nation out of the Great Depression. Roosevelt and his government developed projects that would put people back to work. Over several years, the New Deal brought new roads, parks, airports, bridges, and schools to California. With these new job opportunities, people began to make some money

and get back on their feet. Two projects that had major effects on California were the Hoover Dam and the Golden Gate Bridge.

You might wonder what the Hoover Dam has to do with California. It's not even in California—it's on the border between Nevada and Arizona. Even though the dam is located more than 250 miles from Los Angeles, it provides major benefits to the city and to many other parts of Southern California. The dam, completed in 1936, was built to control the unpredictable Colorado River. The river often flooded in the spring, and sometimes dried up completely in the summer. By controlling the river, floods could be prevented, and water could be used to irrigate crops in normally dry areas.

LET THE GAMES BEGIN!

The Olympic Summer Games held in Los Angeles in 1932 almost didn't happen. In the midst of the Great Depression, California officials worried—would athletes come? Would spectators?

As it turned out, officials had nothing to worry about. More than 100,000 people flocked to the opening ceremonies. They wanted to see the grand Memorial Coliseum and the other amazing facilities built especially for the Olympic games.

Even though only half as many athletes competed in events like wrestling, track and field, swimming, water polo, hockey, and fencing, competition was fierce—numerous world records were broken. Even though a depression gripped the country, California made the decision to go for the gold, and most would agree that the Golden State was a medal winner!

(left) A view of the Golden Gate Bridge looking north from the south tower. *National Oceanic and Atmospheric Administration/Rich Bourgerie*

(right) A view of the Hoover Dam after it was completed in 1936. The dam spans the Colorado River between Nevada and Arizona. *United States Bureau of Land Reclamation, P45-300-01501*

Today the dam also supplies drinking water to places like Los Angeles and San Diego. In fact, if you've ever sipped water from a fountain at Disneyland or San Diego's SeaWorld, you've tasted water from the Colorado River and Lake Mead, the large reservoir created by the dam.

Additionally, the dam provides hydroelectric power to areas such as Arizona, Nevada, and California. The force of the water that flows through giant pipes at the dam creates energy. Generators then harness that energy to produce electricity. Almost 60 percent of the electricity produced at the Hoover Dam goes directly to California.

So, if you're a Californian, the next time you're drinking a cool glass of water on a hot day or watching your favorite television show, you might want to salute the 21,000 men who worked

24 hours a day, 7 days a week, for 5 years to build the Hoover Dam.

Another major project built during the Depression years was San Francisco's Golden Gate Bridge. In the early part of the 20th century, San Francisco had growing pains. Surrounded on three sides by water, the city in many ways felt closed in. As the population increased, and as more and more people began driving automobiles, it became more difficult for people to get around.

People needed a quick and easy way to travel north from San Francisco to cities in Marin County such as San Rafael and Novato. Ferry systems helped, but long lines of traffic often congested the areas near the ferry as people tried to make their way across the Golden Gate, the strait between the San Francisco Bay and the Pacific Ocean. San Franciscan officials knew they needed to do something. The city needed a way to link with the lesser-populated counties of northern California.

By 1933, the time had come—San Francisco was ready to build a major bridge. And the Golden Gate Bridge wouldn't be just any old bridge; it would be a modern technological marvel. Many Californians were in favor of the bridge, but most seriously wondered if such a project could be successfully built. To reach from one shore to the other, the bridge would have to span about 4,000 feet—no other bridges of that length existed at that time. Not only that, bridge workers would have to face dangerous conditions such as fog, storms, and high winds. Even so, San Franciscans were determined.

Construction began in January 1933, and the bridge was completed four years later. The finished product was breathtaking. People couldn't wait to cross the massive steel and concrete structure. And on May 27, 1937, they had their chance. About 200,000 people crossed the bridge that day. Some walked, some ran, some rode bicycles, and others skated. And a few more creative souls made their way across by tap dancing or walking on stilts! The next day, the first cars made their way across the span. The bridge's chief engineer, Joseph Strauss, wrote a poem to commemorate the event. The poem's first line read, "At last, the mighty task is done."

President Roosevelt's New Deal put people back to work and helped them slowly pull out of the Depression. Some of California's New Deal projects include the murals inside San Francisco's Coit Tower, the Eureka Courthouse, the Yuba Bridge, Newport Beach Elementary School, and the stone amphitheater at John Hinkel Park in Berkeley.

As the nation continued to work to pull out of the Depression, another major event occurred: World War II. It was a war that would shape the lives of Californians and people all over the world.

WHY IS THE GOLDEN GATE BRIDGE ORANGE?

This is an often-asked question, and it has a rather complicated answer. A major debate raged when trying to decide on the perfect color. One idea was gray, but some worried that if painted gray, the bridge wouldn't stand out in the fog. The air force wanted orange and white stripes, while the navy pushed for yellow and black stripes. Both wanted something that would be easily visible. The debate raged. Black would make the structure look smaller, and a silver color would make the bridge look flimsy. Officials finally decided on International Orange. It was a color that would make the bridge stand out yet still mesh with the surroundings.

Wartime California

On the morning of December 7, 1941, Japanese bombers flew over the Hawaiian Islands. In a surprise attack, the Japanese bombed US Navy ships and airfields in Pearl Harbor, killing more than 2,000 Americans and wounding more than 1,000. The following day, the United States declared war on Japan. America's involvement in World War II had begun.

The attack on Pearl Harbor shocked and frightened Americans, and it worried Californians even more. Since California lies directly across the Pacific Ocean from Japan, Californians felt they were at especially high risk for Japanese attacks. When reports came in of Japanese submarines torpedoing ships off the California coast, residents became even more concerned. California's major cities of Los Angeles, San Francisco, and San Diego seemed to be easy targets for the Japanese. Thankfully, these cities were never directly attacked.

The war brought many changes to California's people and economy. In order to successfully fight the war, the United States needed vital equipment such as ships and airplanes. Since some of the leading aircraft manufacturers had plants in Los Angeles and San Diego, it made sense that these plants would expand during the war. Also, when President Roosevelt realized the great need for ships, he contacted California businessman Henry Kaiser. Kaiser had never built a ship before, but he was a man who knew how to get things done. Workers for aircraft manufacturers like Douglas and Lockheed and in shipyards in Richmond, Vallejo, Oakland, and other areas worked 24 hours a day to produce the necessary supplies and equipment for the US military.

These industries grew so quickly that California found itself without enough workers to fill all the positions. With so many men off fighting the war, manufacturers had to look elsewhere to find employees. As word got out that these industries needed workers, people, particularly African Americans from the rural South, flocked to the coast. Even though they had previously been discriminated against, many African Americans got jobs building ships and planes during World War II.

Women also started working in these industries, even though these types of factory jobs had

Men rolling out a completed Douglas A-20 attack bomber at a Long Beach, California, assembly plant (1942). *Franklin D. Roosevelt Library Digital Archives*

always been considered "men's work." The women welded, manufactured guns, repaired planes, and attached plates to ships with fasteners called rivets. Due to the work they performed, it is no surprise these women were given the nickname "Rosie the Riveter." By 1943 almost one-half of the aircraft workers and about one-quarter of the shipbuilders in Southern California were women.

People of different races and genders united to become part of the war effort. This pulling together of various groups changed the way people interacted with one another. A great sense of pride filled Californians during this time. One group, however, suffered severely because of the war.

Japanese Internment

After the bombing of Pearl Harbor, many Californians and other Americans thought that the Japanese people living in the United States were a threat to their safety. They saw anyone of Japanese ancestry as an enemy and feared that the Japanese might act as spies or try to attack American cities from within. To prevent this from happening, President Franklin D. Roosevelt signed an order that would send Japanese people to internment camps in California, Arkansas, Arizona, Utah, and other states.

Imagine how you would feel if the government suddenly told you and your family that you had only a few days to decide what you were going to do with your home, your car, your pets, and almost all of your possessions. Imagine packing up only the few things that you could carry and

World War II poster showing the necessity of women workers to the war effort (1942). *Northwestern University Library*

being shipped off on a truck, bus, or train and not knowing when or if you would return home. Not only did the Japanese lose their homes and land, many were also separated from their families.

Two of the government-established relocation camps were built at Manzanar and Tule Lake, California. Barbed wire fences stretched around large housing units called barracks. The Japanese lived as prisoners in these camps with little or no privacy. The often-overcrowded barracks had electricity, but no running water. Families were sometimes separated within the camps,

Headlines of a February 1942 *San Francisco Examiner* announce the removal of California Japanese to internment camps.
Library of Congress, LC-USZ62-17121

Making Amends

Sometimes people do things that they believe are right at the time, but later realize they made a serious mistake. This is what happened concerning the Japanese relocation during World War II. After the bombing of Pearl Harbor, Americans were genuinely afraid. Nothing like that had ever happened before. The United States had never been attacked in that way. People let their fear override their humanity. Many Americans saw all people of Japanese ancestry, even if they were born in America, as a threat or an enemy. This regrettable mindset is what set the relocation camps into motion.

It took years for the government and the American people to realize that a terrible mistake had been made. About 50 years after the internees' release, the US Congress passed the Civil Liberties Act of 1988. The act apologized for the "grave injustice" that had been done to those forced into the camps. As a way of making amends, the US government eventually paid $20,000 to each surviving Japanese American affected by the camps. While the money acted as a small repayment for the immense suffering they endured, not all Japanese internees received their share because many had died before the act passed in 1988.

The Great Depression and World War II took their toll on California and the nation, but as always, Californians and the American people were ready to begin again.

the internees' mail was read before they received it, and they had to stand in long lines for their meals. Rosie Kakuuchi, an internee held at Manzanar, said, "One of the hardest things to endure was the communal latrines, with no partitions; and showers with no stalls."

Even with these difficult conditions, the Japanese people tried to make the best of the situation. Schools, churches, sports, and movies were offered in some of the camps, but these things made life only a little easier. Most internees remained at the camps for two or more years before being released at the end of the war.

Japanese and Japanese Americans being loaded onto a bus at Lone Pine, California, en route to the Manzanar War Relocation Center.
Library of Congress, LC-USZ62-44093

9

Moving Forward

After the war, California continued to grow and prosper. New opportunities existed for those who worked in aerospace, agriculture, and various other industries. Superhighways packed with cars and trucks connected cities, and large, new residential communities sprouted up across the landscape.

By the early 1960s California was home to more people than in any other state in the United States. By the 1970s and '80s, development slowed somewhat, but the state's population continued to grow. In 2009 more than 36 million people called California home.

Let's Go to the Park!

Between 1955 and 1965, two major tourist attractions became established in California—theme parks! On July 17, 1955, Walt Disney opened Disneyland—"The Place Where Dreams Come True"—in Anaheim. Among other activities, early Disney visitors dodged wild animals on the Jungle Cruise, giggled with Dumbo the Flying Elephant, and squealed, rocked, and rolled on the Matterhorn, the first-of-its-kind, tubular steel rollercoaster. The cost of admission on opening day was $1.00 for adults and $0.50 for children under 12. More than 25,000 people took advantage of those low prices.

Los Angeles skyline at dusk taken from behind the Griffith Observatory.
Steve Minkler

And that was only the beginning. In 2008, more than 14 million people walked through those gates. Think how many Mickey ears may have been sold since Disney's beginnings!

Another magical, yet fishy, park opened only a few years later in San Diego. In the early 1960s four friends who went to school at the University of California–Los Angeles had an idea. They wanted to build a restaurant—but not just an ordinary eating establishment. The men wanted to build a restaurant where diners could view underwater life.

Their idea didn't work out quite as planned, but lucky for us, they thought of another way to share the joys of the ocean. In 1964, SeaWorld made waves in California with its dolphins, sea lions, and saltwater aquariums. Only a short time later, visitors could also view seals, penguins, and even an orca.

Today, more than four million people visit SeaWorld each year. And it's a good thing. Sea World needs to keep the dollars coming in to feed all their critters. Bottle-nosed dolphins eat 25 to 30 pounds of fish each day, and manatees can munch more than 150 pounds of romaine lettuce every day—and that's on top of their carrot, apple, and sweet potato snacks.

Play Ball!

Another major pastime also boomed during this period: sports. California is home to dozens of professional baseball, football, basketball, hockey, and soccer teams. As early as 1959, the Los Angeles Dodgers were knocking it out of the park to earn California's very first World Series title. And the Oakland A's three-peat World Series titles in 1972, '73, and '74 can't be overlooked either.

When it comes to the pigskin, California teams have had their share of victories, too. The Oakland Raiders brought home California's first league championship in Super Bowl XI in 1977. And almost 20 years later, two Golden State teams treated the nation to an all-California Super Bowl when the San Francisco 49ers defeated the San Diego Chargers 49–26.

If you're talking about California sports, you definitely can't forget basketball. The world famous Los Angeles Lakers have rocked the National Basketball Association with 10—count 'em, 10!—NBA Championships since 1971. MVPs Wilt Chamberlain, Magic Johnson, Kareem Abdul-Jabbar, Shaquille O'Neal, and Kobe Bryant

Two whales leap from the water at SeaWorld San Diego. *Steve Minkler*

have all the moves to show the other teams how it's done. And when it comes to basketball, we can't skip the women. The Los Angeles Sparks were WNBA champs in 2001 and 2002, and the Sacramento Monarchs led the pack in 2005.

For those interested in goalies and pucks, who can forget when the Anaheim Ducks skated to victory in 2007 to bring home the NHL's Stanley Cup? That calls for a *quack*!

And you don't want to neglect those who have an interest in dribbling, headers, and bicycle kicks. The San Jose Earthquakes emerged victorious in the 2001 and 2003 Major League Soccer Championships. In 2002 and 2005, it was the Los Angeles Galaxy's turn to hoist the MLS Cup. Go, team!

Let's Get High Tech

Have you ever played a video game? Surfed the Web? Chatted on a cell phone? If you have, you've used a computer chip. And chances are, that chip was produced in Silicon Valley. In the 1970s and 1980s, Silicon Valley, located in the southern part of the San Francisco Bay area, emerged as the leader in computer technology.

Some of the first major projects to come out of Silicon Valley were developed by Bill Hewlett and Dave Packard. With only a little more than $500 in their pockets, Hewlett and Packard (now most widely known as HP) helped begin the digital age. The men's work first began in a garage in Palo Alto where they built an electronic instrument that checked sound equipment. These audio oscillators were first purchased by the Walt Disney companies and used in theaters when showing such movies as *Fantasia*. Over time, the HP company they built developed pocket calculators, computers, computer printers, scanners, and other equipment.

One of the most well-known Silicon Valley companies is Apple, Inc. Two Steves, Steve Wozniak and Steve Jobs, came together to start a personal computer revolution. At 22, Wozniak worked for HP. And before Jobs was 20, he had designed video games for Atari. Jobs knew a market existed for personal computers—PCs—easy-to-use computers people could use in their own homes. He pushed Wozniak to design and build such a computer, and Wozniak did just that. They called the machine Apple I.

The men needed money to get their business off the ground; so Jobs sold his Volkswagen microbus, and Wozniak sold his favorite programmable calculator to help with the start-up. Over time, Wozniak continued to improve upon that first PC while Jobs focused on the business side of things. By 1978, Apple II was released, and the rest, as they say, is history.

Today, Apple and all its "i's"—iPhone, iTunes, iPod, and its latest iPad—are off-the-charts when it comes to sales numbers. As of 2010, Apple has sold 50 million iPhones and 35 million iPod Touches, and users have downloaded more than 10 billion iTunes songs. Apple, along with Silicon Valley companies such as Intel, HP, Yahoo!, Google, and eBay have changed the way we work, play, and go about our daily lives.

Tough Times for the Golden State

For all the good things that happened during this time period, some negatives also occurred. Even during the 1960s, groups of people in California and across the United States were still being discriminated against. Many African Americans were not allowed to buy houses in white neighborhoods. Some employers would not hire them. African American children could only attend certain schools. During this time, protests began

César Chávez (1927–93) at a 1982 United Farm Workers meeting in San Jose. *San Jose State University, Special Collections & Archives, Ted Sahl Collection*

to erupt. Those discriminated against were tired of being treated unfairly.

Some of the protests were peaceful—people just did what they could to make themselves heard. They marched in the streets carrying posters or wrote letters to public officials.

Sadly, other protests became violent. One such protest occurred in the Los Angeles neighborhood of Watts. In 1965 about 90 percent of the people who lived in Watts were black, but many of the area businesses had white owners. On a steamy August night, a white policeman pulled over a car to arrest a black man they believed to be driving while intoxicated. The encounter grew violent and sparked a massive riot. Over the course of six days, an estimated 35,000 angry blacks threw rocks, bottles, bricks, and chunks of concrete through store windows. They overturned cars, burned buildings, and stole property from the damaged businesses. Local police and the National Guard were sent in to control the riot, but by the time the ruckus was over, 34 people had died, more than 1,000 had been injured, and 4,000 had been arrested.

The riots were an ugly part of California history. Thankfully, changes began taking place during this time that would help minorities enjoy the rights they deserved.

César Chávez

African Americans weren't the only people discriminated against in the 1960s. Migrant farmworkers, often Mexicans or Mexican Americans who came to California to look for work, were also treated unfairly. They toiled day after day under a scorching sun, picking peas, beans, cotton, grapes, tomatoes, and other crops. Employers paid them very little—sometimes only 25 to 50 cents for each basket they picked. Most farmworkers lived in their cars or in run-down shacks that were often rented from farm owners at very high prices.

A man named César Chávez was quite aware of these poor living and working conditions. As a 10-year-old, he constantly moved with his family from place to place to find work in the fields. This was the only way he and his family could survive.

As he grew older, Chávez never forgot his childhood experiences. Chávez knew he wanted to do something to help migrant workers. He began traveling around talking to workers and banding them together. Chávez believed that if the workers came together as a group, they might be able to make changes in their lives.

In 1962 Chávez started an organization called the National Farm Workers Association (NFWA), an organization that later became known as the United Farm Workers (UFW). Chávez worked long hours helping his organization grow into an important labor union. Labor unions are groups of workers who come together to fight for fair wages and better working conditions.

In 1965 grape pickers in Delano, California, made only one dollar per hour. How could they feed their families on such a small amount? It was time to take action. NFWA members made a decision: *¡Huelga!* (WEL-gah). The grape pickers were going on strike. They refused to enter the fields until they were treated more fairly and received better pay.

DOLORES HUERTA

In the early 1950s, Dolores Huerta taught elementary school in California. Each school day, Huerta became troubled because so many of her students came to school hungry and wearing tattered clothing. Huerta knew she was helping her students by teaching them, but she wanted to do more. She left her teaching job and fought to make sure Mexican Americans had the right to vote and that they were not discriminated against.

In 1962, Huerta joined César Chávez in founding the United Farm Workers. She helped organize the 1965 Delano Grape Strike and worked tirelessly for the rights of all people. When it came to civil rights, Chávez and Huerta never gave up on the UFW's motto, *"¡Sí se puede!"* (see say PWAY-day)—"Yes, it can be done!"

At first, the strike did little good. Vineyard owners refused to give in. Later, however, when some of the NFWA marched about 300 miles to Sacramento, people outside of California became more aware of the conditions the grape pickers faced. Chávez called for people across America to stop buying and eating grapes. This action, called a boycott, got the vineyard owners' attention. The owners couldn't make any money if people weren't buying their product. Finally, by 1970, the owners gave in to the worker's demands for better pay and working conditions. This was the first of Chávez's many victories.

In one of his speeches, Chávez said, "Stop and think: What do you dream of as you work day after day in the hot sun? You dream of a nicer home for your wife, a good school for your kids,

The portion of the San Francisco-Oakland Bay Bridge that collapsed after the Loma Prieta earthquake in 1989. *US Department of the Interior/US Geological Survey/C. E. Meyer*

some dignity and rest for the older ones. Those have always been the dreams of the farm workers, but they never started to come true until we built this union."

Chávez spent the remainder of his life fighting for farm workers' rights. Sadly, conditions for farmworkers still aren't always as they should be, but a step in the right direction was achieved through Chávez's work.

Air Pollution

Unfortunately, when many people think of Los Angeles, they think of smog, a type of air pollution caused by sunlight's reaction to gases produced by factories and automobiles. Smog was first recognized in the Los Angeles area in the early 1940s, and as more and more cars came into use, the smog only got worse. By 2006, California had more than 33 million registered vehicles, the most of any state. And almost all of those cars, trucks, boats, and other vehicles are dirtying the air with the gases they emit.

Power plants, factories, gas stations, and even our homes are also sources of air pollution. One of the reasons smog is so common in California has to do with the state's physical features. Many of California's cities are located in valley areas where air pollution settles and becomes trapped. The surrounding mountains hold in the pollution and do not allow the air to properly circulate.

Smog can cause many health problems including itchy, burning eyes; scratchy throats; and more serious problems such as asthma and bronchitis. Thankfully, California government officials put plans such as the California Clean Air Act (1980) in place to help reduce the amount of air pollution. Today, the California Air Resources Board performs research, monitors smog levels, and helps enforce pollutant regulations. But even with these steps, smog still continues to be a problem.

Forces of Nature

On October 17, 1989, 5:04 P.M.—half an hour before the first pitch of the World Series game between the Oakland A's and the San Francisco Giants would clear home plate—there was a rumble. Some of the players thought excited fans were shaking Candlestick Park with the stomping of their feet. But when the shaking became more intense, the realization hit: earthquake! One fan noted as she sat in the stands, "I remember . . . watching the rolling waves of seats . . . who'd have thought that concrete would roll?"

Two significant earthquakes shook and swayed California in the late 1980s and early 1990s, both leaving massive destruction in their wake. The 6.9 magnitude quake that occurred just before the World Series game was centered near Mount Loma Prieta in the Santa Cruz Mountains. Although the tremor lasted only 15 seconds, the downtowns of Santa Cruz, Oakland, and the San Francisco Bay areas were severely affected. A large section of the San Francisco Bay Bridge fell, and the Cypress Street overpass on the Nimitz Freeway (I-880) collapsed. Buildings were destroyed both by the quake and by resulting fires. More than 60 people died, and the quake did more than $6 billion in property damage.

Only a few years later, in 1994, the Northridge earthquake abruptly woke people from their sleep when it shook the San Fernando Valley region of Southern California. Shopping centers, parking garages, houses, apartments, and roadways were destroyed in the 6.7 magnitude quake. More than 50 people were killed as a result of this disaster.

Sadly, earthquakes aren't the only kinds of natural disasters to plague California. Another serious problem is wildfires. Thick smoke fills the air, stinging eyes and noses. Ash drifts down like snowflakes. Schools and businesses close. Thousands pack up what belongings they can carry and flee their homes.

Wildfires can be caused by droughts, lightning strikes, and humans who accidentally or purposely set fires. Another condition that makes California particularly at risk for wildfires is the Santa Ana winds. Each fall and early winter, these scorching winds blow westward from the desert. The winds make the underbrush even drier and therefore more prone to burning. Also, when a fire occurs, the 50 to 60 mph and higher winds cause the flames to spread even faster.

Two major fires in recent California history occurred in October 2003 and July 2007. The first series of fires, known as the Cedar wildfires, devastated parts of San Diego County, burning more than 270,000 acres. Firefighters worked tirelessly to put out the fires and save homes, but the fires destroyed or damaged more than 2,800 structures. Fifteen people, including a firefighter, lost their lives in the blaze. One of the fires in the Cedar blazes began when a lost hunter tried to signal rescuers by starting a fire. Sadly, arson was

PROTECTING PETS

When people are faced with a disaster such as a wildfire, they immediately think of taking care of themselves and their families. But there are other precious parts of their lives that they'd never forget—their pets. When one evacuee of the 2007 San Diego wildfires looked for a place to go, she worried: "I have to find someplace to accept two dogs, two cats, and a turtle."

Thankfully, during these fires, several plans were put in place for people with pets. Organizations like the Humane Society and local departments of animal services pitched in to make animals feel at home. Food, water, and pet crates were provided, areas outside of Qualcomm Stadium were set aside for larger pets, and the MUTT Mobile was on hand to provide medical care.

the cause of some of the other Cedar fires—these fires were set on purpose.

In 2007 another wildfire struck San Diego County. These fires, known as the Witch fires because they began near Witch Creek Canyon, charred almost 200,000 acres and damaged or destroyed more than 1,500 structures. Almost one million people had to be evacuated from their homes. One San Diego resident noted, "Everyone is running around scared. No one knows what to do. There is no place to go. I have no place to go."

MAKE AN AIR POLLUTION LOGBOOK

Many areas of California are known for smoggy skies. It's important for us to do what we can to help reduce air pollution. To help keep up with your contributions to clean air, make a logbook to record what you've done.

Materials

Cardboard cereal box

Scissors

Pencil

Ruler

Hole Punch

10 sheets of notebook or copy paper (look for paper that says "Recycled" on the label)

Short pieces of yarn, ribbon, raffia, old shoestrings, or something similar to bind your logbook

Markers

☛ Cut off the front and back panels from an empty cereal box. For your cover, take one of the cardboard pieces and mark a light line with your pencil about ¾ inch from the front cover's left edge.

Align a ruler next to the line and run your scissors lightly down the line. This will help your cover open more easily.

Put the two pieces of cardboard together. Punch two holes near the top, two holes near the middle, and two holes near the bottom. Place the paper between the covers and use the covers as a guide to punch holes in the paper. You may have to trim the paper's edges so it will fit within the covers.

Using the string, raffia, yarn, or other material, thread one short piece through each hole and tie in a loose knot. Gently open your front cover and fold it on the crease you made with the scissors. Decorate the cover with the markers.

You may also wish to use your book to record the air quality in your area. Daily reports of the Air Quality Index can be found for many cities at the US Environmental Protection Agency's AirNow website (www.airnow.gov), at the California Environmental Protection Agency Air Resources Board website (www.arb.ca.gov), or from you local news outlets.

To use your logbook, look at the list of things you can do to help the air quality in your community. For each entry, write the date, what you did (use the list here), and place a check mark beside the activity. You will also want to record activities where you didn't make the best decisions when it came to air pollution—such as not turning off a light when you left a room or forgetting to recycle a plastic water bottle. Next to these entries, make an X.

At the end of the week, count up how many check marks and how many Xs you have. If you have more checks than Xs, good for you. Do something to celebrate!

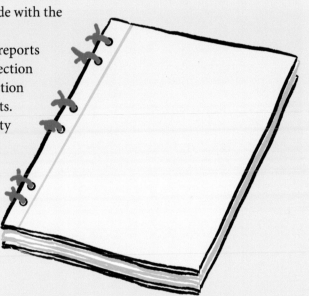

THINGS YOU CAN DO TO HELP PREVENT AIR POLLUTION

> Turn off lights, televisions, computers, etc. when not in use.

> Bike or walk whenever possible instead of riding in a car.

> If you have to ride, take a bus or carpool.

> Find out about recycling in your city and then RECYCLE!

> When shopping, try to buy products with the "Recycled" label.

> Plant trees—they help clean the air.

> Talk to your friends and family about the importance of keeping our air clean.

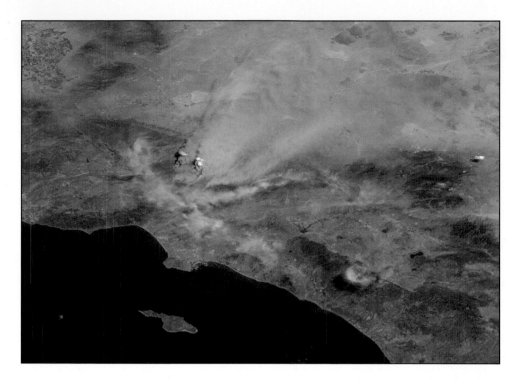

A view of a California wildfire as captured from space in August 2009. *NASA/JPL-Caltech*

Some evacuees were able to rent hotel rooms. Others stayed with family or friends. Around 20,000 evacuees sheltered at Qualcomm Stadium, the home of the San Diego Chargers. Sleeping on cots or in tents within the complex while worrying about their homes must have been difficult, but relief organizations and volunteers did everything they could to make their temporary guests comfortable. They provided food, water, newspapers, blankets, and even massages. Clowns and balloon artists roamed the center entertaining the children. Even though these Californians faced nature's uncontrollable wrath, they made the best of the situation they had.

Troubled Government, Troubled Economy

In the early part of the new millennium, California faced numerous political and economic challenges. The people of California had lost confidence in their state governor, Gray Davis. During Davis's administration, residents thought taxes were too high, and most believed the schools weren't meeting the needs of their children. The state also began dealing with energy issues. Power outages known as rolling blackouts led to periods where electricity would go out in a particular area for a limited time. These rolling blackouts helped reduce energy usage when the power supply dipped too low. Additionally, the state of California's budget was a mess because they were spending more money than they had coming in. In short, Californians believed Davis had badly managed their state.

In 2003, California voters decided they were ready for a change. They went to the polls and voted to recall Governor Davis. A recall is a way to remove an official from office before his or her term expires. Davis's recall made history—no other California governor had ever been removed from office by a recall vote.

As voters made their decisions on the recall, they also faced another task. They had to elect someone to take Davis's place. Who could help them out of their troubles? they wondered. Who would make the best leader for their state?

More than 130 candidates hoped to become California's governor in 2003, but only one winner could emerge. Voters chose former body-building champion and Hollywood film star Arnold Schwarzenegger as California's 38th governor. In his acceptance speech, Schwarzenegger said he knew that hard work would make California a better place—"I believe in the people of California, and I know that together we can do great things."

As governor, Schwarzenegger worked on programs that would repair California's economy, improve its environment, and help put people back to work. Unfortunately, most of these programs were unsuccessful. The people of California continued to face major budget, education, unemployment, and environmental issues. Schwarzenegger was reelected to a second term in 2006, but after seven years as California's governor, he left office in January 2011.

California still struggles, but the dream of a better, healthier, happier Golden State lives on.

IT'S POLITICS!

California has connections to the United States presidency. Do you know what they are?

➤ Herbert Hoover, the nation's 31st president, graduated from Stanford University in 1895 with a degree in geology.

➤ The 37th president of the United States, Richard M. Nixon, was born in Yorba Linda in 1913. As a boy, he worked at his father's gas station and store in Whittier.

➤ Our 40th president, Ronald Reagan, wasn't a California native, but he had a Hollywood career. After high school, Reagan headed for the Golden State and appeared in more than 50 films. He later served two terms as governor of California.

Working Toward a Brighter Tomorrow

Throughout California's long history, people of widely varied ethnic backgrounds have come from all over the world to make the Golden State their home. Asians, African Americans, Hispanics, Caucasians, and countless others came seeking their dreams.

Sadly, some newcomers faced hardship and discrimination. Some still face these issues today. Californians are used to adversity, however, whether from unfair treatment, earthquakes, fires, or political, economic, or environmental issues; Californians know how to fight back.

They know how to build and how to rebuild. They know how to improve their lives and the lives of others. As the people of California move through the coming years, they will no doubt face their share of hard times along with the good times. But, working together, they will bounce back, better and stronger than before.

Who knows what California's future holds? Who knows what triumphs and difficulties Californians will face in upcoming years? No one knows for sure, but throughout history, the California dream has endured. As Californians work together, they'll hold tight to that dream and embrace the uniqueness that make Californians and the Golden State like none other.

Resources

If you want to learn more about California's history, people, and culture, take a look at these books, websites, and places to visit.

Books

*Ambrose, Stephen E. *The Transcontinental Railroad: A Primary Source History of America's First Coast-to-Coast Railroad*. New York: Rosen, 2003.

*Anderson, Dale. *The California Missions*. Milwaukee: World Almanac Library, 2002.

*Ansary, Mir Tamim. *California History, 2nd edition*. Chicago: Heinemann, 2010.

*Blumberg, Rhoda. *The Great American Gold Rush*. New York: Bradbury Press, 1989.

Conlan, Roberta, ed. *The Indians of California*. Alexandria, VA: Time-Life Books, 1994.

Holliday, J. S. *The World Rushed In: An Eyewitness Account of a Nation Heading West*. New York: Simon and Schuster, 1981.

Rawls, James J. and Walton Bean. *California: An Interpretive History*. New York: McGraw Hill, 2008.

*Rosinsky, Natalie M. *California Ranchos*. Minneapolis: Compass Point Books, 2006.

*Stanley, Jerry. *Hurry Freedom: African Americans in Gold Rush California*. New York: Crown Publishers, 2000.

Starr, Kevin. *California: A History*. New York: Modern Library/ Random House, 2005.

Books marked with a * are especially appropriate for younger readers.

Websites to Explore

California Historical Society

www.californiahistoricalsociety.org

This website provides a thorough overview of California's history on its "California History Online" page that covers the 1600s through the 1900s. Student and teacher resources can also be found on the site, which includes a comprehensive list of other sites to explore.

Calisphere

www.calisphere.universityofcalifornia.edu

This University of California site is jam-packed with primary source information about California. Search for photographs, diaries, documents, and more, or browse the in-depth "Themed Collections," which take you directly to resources on such topics as the gold rush, the Great Depression, social issues, and others.

Learn California

www.learncalifornia.org

An amazing site about all things California, created by the California State Archives. Students and teachers alike can delve into California history using the primary resources such as the letters, images, and historical records found on these pages. Be sure to visit the "Online Exhibits" page to discover more information about California missions, the 1906 earthquake, notable Californian African Americans, and more.

PBS American Experience

Gold Rush: www.pbs.org/wgbh/amex/goldrush/
Transcontinental Railroad: www.pbs.org/wgbh/amex/tcrr/
The Donner Party: www.pbs.org/wgbh/americanexperience/films/ donner/
Dust Bowl: www.pbs.org/wgbh/americanexperience/films/dustbowl/
Hoover Dam: www.pbs.org/wgbh/americanexperience/films/hoover/

American Experience, an outstanding series from PBS, has covered many California-related topics. The site presents maps, time lines, activities, and biographies on the gold rush, the transcontinental railroad, the Donner Party, the Dust Bowl, and the Hoover Dam, to name a few. If you're searching for information in other areas, use the search box to check for additional topics and events.

The Virtual Museum of the City of San Francisco

www.sfmuseum.org

Some of the major exhibits covered by the site include the Chinese during the gold rush, the Great Earthquake and Fire, World War II and Japanese internment, and the Golden Gate Bridge. The primary source newspaper articles and images will transport the reader back in time.

Places to Visit

The California Museum

1020 O Street
Sacramento, CA 95814
(916) 653-7524
www.californiamuseum.org

This unique museum focuses on both the people and the events of California history. In 2006 California First Lady Maria Shriver established the museum's Hall of Fame to recognize the achievements of notable Californians. Check out the online exhibit "California Legacy Trails" to find out more about the fascinating people and places of the Golden State.

California State Indian Museum

2618 K Street
Sacramento, CA 95816
(916) 324-0971
www.parks.ca.gov/default.asp?page_id=486

If you want to learn more about California's native people, this is the place. View exhibits, photographs, baskets, and clothing, and try your hand at using Native American tools.

California State Railroad Museum

125 I Street
Sacramento, CA 95814
(916) 445-6645
www.csrmf.org

This is a don't-miss museum when it comes to California history. It's no surprise that more than 500,000 people visit the museum each year. Visitors can view restored locomotives and train cars, discover interesting information about the First Transcontinental Railroad and its impact on Chinese and other immigrant workers, and find out more about California agriculture and farm workers.

The George C. Page Museum and La Brea Pits

5801 Wilshire Boulevard
Los Angeles, CA 90036
(323) 934-7243
www.tarpits.org

Located in Hancock Park near downtown Los Angeles, this fascinating museum houses fossils and complete skeletons of creatures excavated from the tar pits. Take a walk throughout the park to see the pits themselves. During the summer, visitors often have the opportunity to watch actual excavations.

Japanese American National Museum

369 E. First Street
Los Angeles, CA 90012
(213) 625-0414
www.janm.org

Located in Little Tokyo, near downtown Los Angeles, this museum is dedicated to preserving the history and culture of Japanese Americans. One of its major areas of focus is the life of Japanese Americans before, during, and after World War II.

The Latino Museum of History, Art, and Culture

514 S. Spring Street
Los Angeles, CA 90013
(213) 626-7600
www.thelatinomuseum.org

At this museum, you can celebrate the incredible creations of Latino artists and delve into Latino and Chicano history and heritage through books, film, documents, and more. Biographies of many of the artists are included on the website.

Marshall Gold Discovery State Historic Park
310 Back Street
Coloma, CA 95613
(530) 622-3470
www.parks.ca.gov/default.asp?page_id=484
Want to see where James Marshall first discovered gold on the American River? This is the place. Take a look at a replica of Sutter's Mill, and don't forget to try your hand at panning some gold of your own.

Museum of Tolerance
Simon Wiesenthal Plaza
9786 W. Pico Boulevard
Los Angeles, CA 90035
(310) 553-8403
www.museumoftolerance.com
This exceptional museum strives to raise awareness about prejudice and racism not only in California but throughout the world. Visit the Action Lab either in person or online to find out how you can get involved to make the world a more peaceful, understanding place.

San Juan Bautista Mission and State Historic Park
406 Second Street
San Juan Bautista, CA 95045
(831) 623-4528
www.oldmissionsjb.org
There are many missions that can be toured along the Camino Real, but the San Juan Bautista Mission and Park are especially notable. Take a tour of the mission itself, or explore the plaza's stables, hotel, blacksmith shop, and jail.

The Tech Museum
201 S. Market Street
San Jose, CA 95113
(408) 294-8324
www.thetech.org
This museum focuses on the technological advances of Silicon Valley. If science and technology is your thing, you won't want to miss these interactive programs and exhibits. If you can't make it to the museum, try out some of the activities in the "Online Fun" section of the website.

Index

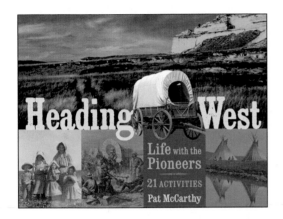

978-1-55652-809-5
$16.95 (CAN $18.95)
Also available in e-book formats

Heading West
Life with the Pioneers, 21 Activities

Pat McCarthy

Tracing the vivid saga of Native American and pioneer men, women, and children, this guide covers the colonial beginnings of the westward expansion to the last of the homesteaders in the late 20th century.

978-1-55652-455-4
$14.95 (CAN $16.95)
Also available in e-book formats

World War II for Kids
A History with 21 Activities

Richard Panchyk
Foreword by Senator John McCain

Selected by the Children's Book Council and the National Council for Social Studies as a Notable Social Studies Trade Book for Young People for 2003

"This well-written, well-researched book belongs on every reference bookshelf in American schools and libraries. It is a must-read book for kids and adults." —*Children's Literature*

"Chicago Review Press is famous for high quality, educational activity books. This adds a much-needed humanizing global perspective to [WWII]." —Lee Littlewood, *Copley News Service*

"Fun reading for adults and kids." —Geri Nikolai, *Rockford Register Star*

978-1-55652-569-8
$17.95 (CAN $25.95)
Also available in e-book formats

Frida Kahlo and Diego Rivera
Their Lives and Ideas, 24 Activities

Carol Sabbeth

"Filled with vibrant four-color reproductions of the artwork discussed." —*The Star-Telegram*

"A must-have for the mini-artist in your house." —*South Florida Sun-Sentinel*

"A good catch for anyone interested in the art of Diego Rivera and Frida Kahlo." —*Kliatt*

"A charming introduction." —*The Virginian-Pilot*

"Richly illustrated." —*Children's Literature*

"An inviting and educational journey." —*BC Parent*

"This creative, colorful book is healthy inspiration for young artists." —*Metro Parent*

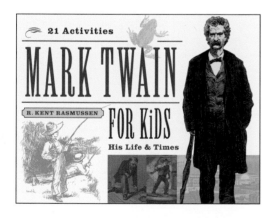

978-1-55652-527-8
$14.95 (CAN $22.95)
Also available in e-book formats

Mark Twain for Kids
His Life & Times, 21 Activities

R. Kent Rasmussen

"This appealing biography will make a useful resource for teachers and student researchers." —*Booklist*

"A useful resource for teachers and student researchers." —*Children's Literature*

"A fun companion to the works of Mr. Twain." —*Dallas Morning News*

CHICAGO REVIEW PRESS

Available at your favorite bookstore, by calling
(800) 888-4741, or at www.chicagoreviewpress.com